chickens, GIN, AND A MAINE FRIENDSHIP

THE CORRESPONDENCE OF

E. B. WHITE

and

EDMUND WARE SMITH

INTRODUCTION BY MARTHA WHITE

Down East Books

CAMDEN, MAINE

Down East Books

Published by Down East Books
An imprint of The Rowman & Littlefield Publishing Group, Inc.
4501 Forbes Blvd., Ste. 200
Lanham, MD 20706
www.rowman.com

Distributed by NATIONAL BOOK NETWORK

*Skidompha
Library*

Published in partnership with Skidompha Public Library
184 Main St, Damariscotta, ME 04543
www.skidompha.org

British Library Cataloguing in Publication Information Available

Library of Congress Cataloging-in-Publication Data
Names: White, Martha, 1954 December 18– writer of introduction. | White, E.
  B. (Elwyn Brooks), 1899–1985. Correspondence. Selections | Smith, Edmund
  Ware, 1900–1967. Correspondence. Selections
Title: Chickens, gin, and a Maine friendship : the correspondence of E. B.
  White and Edmund Ware Smith / introduction by Martha White.
Description: Camden, Maine : Down East Books ; Damariscotta, ME : Skidompha
  Public Library, [2020] | Includes a selection of works by E. B. White
  and Edmund Ware Smith along with their correspondence. | Summary:
  "During the 1950s and 1960s, writers E. B. White and Edmund Ware Smith
  carried on a long correspondence. Introduced by White's granddaughter,
  Martha White, these letters show their first formal communications,
  their chummy middle years, right up to the death of Smith"— Provided by
  publisher.
Identifiers: LCCN 2019059482 (print) | LCCN 2019059483 (ebook) | ISBN
  9781608937325 (hardcover ; alk. paper) | ISBN 9781608937332 (e-book)
Subjects: LCSH: White, E. B. (Elwyn Brooks), 1899–1985—Correspondence. |
  Smith, Edmund Ware, 1900–1967—Correspondence. | Authors, American—20th
  Century—Correspondence.
Classification: LCC PS3545.H5187 Z48 2020 (print) | LCC PS3545.H5187
  (ebook) | DDC 816/.5208—dc23
LC record available at https://lccn.loc.gov/2019059482
LC ebook record available at https://lccn.loc.gov/2019059483

∞™ The paper used in this publication meets the minimum requirements of American National Standard for Information Sciences—Permanence of Paper for Printed Library Materials, ANSI/NISO Z39.48-1992.

Contents

Preface

THE STORY YOU ARE ABOUT TO READ is made only more remarkable by the fact that these letters almost didn't see the light of day. This correspondence between the writers E. B. White and Edmund Ware Smith was generously given to Skidompha Library in Damariscotta, Maine, by E. B. White in 1980, upon the death of Smith's widow, who had lived near the library.

Recognized by the library board as the rare and precious gift that they were, the letters were immediately put under lock and key in the vault of a local bank—and then promptly forgotten. They might be there still if not for the industrious cleaning efforts of bank staff, who discovered and returned several boxes of historical documents to the library in the fall of 2018.

When I first opened the box containing these letters, I thought it was some kind of joke. No one just finds unknown material from one of America's best-known essayists at a small-town library in Maine. And yet here they were.

As I began reading and the two men's correspondence unfolded, I was completely taken by their affection for place (both were transplants to the rugged beauty and idiosyncrasies of Maine) and the warm friendship between them. These men—both literary titans in their own right—had developed a connection through common interests and experiences that start in the formal and round out into the deeply familiar. Here was something not only of another time but also unique. These letters were indeed a rare and precious gift, and the time had come to share them.

I hope that you enjoy their correspondence as much as I did.

—Torie DeLisle,
Skidompha Library

Introduction

IF YOU WERE DOING A STUDY in similarities between E. B. White and Edmund Ware Smith, you could start with words like *author, outdoorsman, amateur husbandman, keen observer,* and that lifelong Maine designation of being "from away." They both moved to Maine mid-career, spent time in Florida but found it wasn't for them, and escaped their offices for the great outdoors as often as possible—White to the Belgrade Lakes and Penobscot Bay and Smith to a log cabin he and his wife built on a lake north of Katahdin and then to Damariscotta. They were birdwatchers, canoeists, small-flock poultrymen, and gin drinkers, and they both enjoyed making things out of wood. They were happily married, enjoyed a good county fair, and preferred houseguests to be of short duration.

Edmund Ware Smith was a natural storyteller and often based his stories on fictionalized versions of the many hunters, fishermen, game wardens, and outdoorsmen he knew, including "Jake's Rangers" from the Damariscotta area. Their exploits were bigger than life, raucous, and generally told in regional vernacular. My grandfather wrote stories but did not voice them. His prose was spare, more formal in grammar and diction, and he was largely an armchair sportsman (although he might pick up a gun if there was a predator at the henhouse, and he enjoyed a fishing rod in a canoe well into his eighties).

Describing his book *Woodsmoke from Old Cabins*, Smith wrote, "In all men in some degree the wilderness wish exists, however hidden in the haste and habit of the world we make. For me, this wish is symbolized and fulfilled by log cabins I have known, built or lived in. I am thinking especially of certain remote cabins sequestered on the banks of rivers or the shores of little-known lakes." For my grandfather, that cabin would have been the one he wrote about in "Once More to the Lake," about his boyhood summers in (and his later return to) the Belgrade Lakes. He was also a fan of Henry David Thoreau's cabin on Walden Pond, and many of his letters (including some of those collected in *Letters of E. B. White*) were written in a similarly austere boathouse on his shore in Maine. Clearly, both Smith and White shared that wilderness wish and enjoyed reading accounts of those who pursued it.

By the time Smith moved to Damariscotta, White had a head start on his saltwater farm up the coast. His chicken coops were well proven, having contributed to the war effort, and my grandfather liked nothing better than to discuss chicken farming and the best way to build a chicken coop or outfit it, so of course they would continue their correspondence. White's introduction for *A Basic Chicken Guide*, reprinted here, is one of my favorites of his essays, with its pithy advice to "Be tidy. Be brave." His letters to Smith detailing the essentials of a chicken coop are as useful today as they were then—and entertaining reading, besides.

Already the two men had shared their love of birdwatching, and songbirds in particular. Smith had published two of White's essays on the subject in the *Ford Times*, "Feeding Station Birds" (1954) and "A Farewell to Wings" (1955), both illustrated by the inimitable Charles Harper. Some of White's descriptions could have as aptly described the two men: "The Chickadee was put on earth to demonstrate the power of positive thinking." And "An early carpenter with but one tool to his kit, the Downy [Wood-pecker] arises at five and goes to work drilling holes, making a bright racket and waking everyone in the neighborhood. . . . In spring, when the sap runs and temptation is strong upon him, the Downy has been known to take a drink."

And there you have it: spreaders of good news and cheer, early risers, carpenters, keen observers, and friends who enjoyed a well-written letter in the mail and a late-afternoon drink, especially along the coast of Maine.

—Martha White,
August 2019

The Correspondence of E. B. White and Edmund Ware Smith

Damariscotta, Maine
November 21, 1956

Dear Mr. White:

Recently, along the route of my happy return from the new Central Staff Office Building of the Ford Company in Dearborn, I stepped into that place in the Grand Central that specializes in cutlery. It's located on the Commodore Bar end of the station's main floor, and is opposite a newsstand. I bought some knives for my wife's birthday present for the Damariscotta kitchen, and then remembered that my suitcase needed repairing. I had heard there was a place in the Grand Central where they do this kind of work, so I said to the cutlery man:

"Where can I get baggage repaired?"

He looked me over pretty carefully and said: "I've heard of a place on Third Avenue, and—"

"But I thought they had a place right here in the station," I said.

And he said: "I don't know of any place here. How many have you got?"

"Just one," I said.

He looked me over pretty carefully again, and said: "Where is it?"

"Up in my room at the Commodore. It's an old bag I've been carrying a long time, and it's kind of worn, and one of the catches—"

"Oh!" he said, with what seemed like relief. "Baggage! I thought you said *daggers!*"

The noise of the station, my faulty articulation due to some recent dental work, a possible slight deafness of the cutlery man all doubtless contributed to the misunderstanding.

But what one of your *New Yorker* pioneers should do is go and talk to that cutlery man, find out just where on Third Avenue they repair daggers, and—what is more important—find out how, or on whom, the daggers were damaged in the first place. This may be one for the police, but I feel the *New Yorker* could handle it all right.

I thought your Wormwood story about the raccoons and other things was very fine. My snooper was over there a second time visiting your neighbor, Waldron, whom I haven't met. Your terrace was reported deserted, and there was a rumor you were commuting between North Brooklin and New York.

The rumble of the snow plow has been heard in the country hereabouts, and the land of the pointed firs is lovely to behold, except for being overrun with deer hunters. Did I tell you this nice old place where we now live was once owned by a man named PickWick? My barn has been repaired, and I am expecting at any moment the delivery of a bench saw and lathe, the backlog of my workshop. I hasten to get this letter finished while I still have fingers.

Yrs.,
Edmund Ware Smith
Damariscotta, Maine

10 December 1956

Dear Mr. Smith:

Third Avenue sounds about right, for dagger repair. But it provided better cover before they ripped the El down. I don't know whether the magazine is going to use your anecdote or not—it has been sent along and perhaps you have heard by now.

Am glad to report that the bricks on my terrace have begun to heave, and some of them have turned green. The cedar windbreak has turned silver. I am trying to turn to gold. The terrace is particularly wonderful in winter because it wears a look of utter desolation—almost unrelieved inutility. If there is such a word. And then, along about February, the woodpile begins to rise into the air, towering above the East Wall and shutting off view of the cove.

As for your bench and lathe, I have promised myself a bench saw as soon as (and not until) I have learned to file a saw. And I guess I would get a lathe, too, if I could learn to sharpen the blade of a plane. The only power tool I have allowed myself is a drill; all the rest of the stuff is going to have to wait till I show signs of becoming a carpenter. My magnum opus, to date, is a little wheelbarrow that I made last winter and spring for my grandson. It is a thing of almost unbelievable beauty and strength. I guess I put in about 100 hours on it, 80 of which were spent looking for materials, applying Band-aids, and standing back to admire.

We're going to be home in North Brooklin for Christmas, if things work out.

Sincerely,
E. B. White

Damariscotta, Maine
March 26, 1957

Dear Mr. White:

To go back to yours of 23 January, my dagger repair item wasn't forwarded to you with commercial intent, but in my then role of free-lance informer. So I can't be disappointed that the boys didn't get excited. I can't be disappointed in anything, at the moment, having just returned from a ten-day stretch in the Central Staff Office Building of the Ford Motor Company, Dearborn, Mich. I am so un-disappointed by my arrival on the South Bristol Road that I am writing this letter at five o'clock in the morning—no doubt the only one you ever had written to you at that hour of day. I wish to report two robins perched on the cedar fence I built, and several crows in a tall spruce that God built. Every now and then a crow or two will sail down from the spruce top for a canapé from my wife's compost pile, which is as big as a drumlin. The sky is red, and I expect that at six o'clock Jake Brophy, our State of Maine Agriculture broadcaster, will be reporting the weather—fringe benefits from the mid-west blizzards, probably.

Charles Harper, the bird man, was in Dearborn while I was there. He came over from Cincinnati with a portfolio of new birds, only they are not new ones. They are old ones—all vanished, or believed to be vanishing, so you can't say with telling affect that you can't write about the passenger pigeon because you never saw one. Who the hell has? You can't default on the grounds that you are unfamiliar with the great auk or the heath hen. Who the hell is?

I think you might feel like giving "Vanished and Vanishing Birds" a whirl, particularly since what you write may very possibly have an influence in retarding, or even preventing, the diminution of those on the list which are surviving or trying to. The list is as follows: Great Auk, Labrador Duck, Passenger Pigeon, Heath Hen, California Condor, Carolina Paroquet, Eskimo Curlew, Ivory-billed Woodpecker, Whooping Crane, Everglade Sail Kite, and Trumpeter Swan.

If any of the birds poses a problem for you, it can be solved by my friend Carl Buchheister, who runs the National Audubon Society headquarters at 1130 Fifth Avenue, your city. If you haven't dropped in there, you ought to anyway. But of course I hope you will do it in the cause of captions for Harper's new set of designs. If you decide to, let me know and I'll send you the colored slides of the bird pictures. The business arrangements would be the same as last time around. Deadline, first week in July.

We've had a couple of good publishers asking to do a book of your captions and the Harper designs, in color. You will be consulted, of course, since the final decision would involve both you and Harper, and also since you retain the rights to whatever you do for our magazines. I think a darned attractive book could be made from this bird series, when we get enough birds and captions.

I meant to write you full instructions on filing a saw, and full congratulations on filing a saw, and full congratulations on your wheelbarrow production for your grandson. But now that I'm down here in civilization, a guy named Clayton Weston does my saw filing. He's good, too. My bench saw and lathe, so far, have produce a handsome settle, a drop-leaf coffee table, some superb cupboards in the back entry, and a dining-room table of incomparable grace and beauty. As I graduate from pine into the hardwoods, all fingers are intact, and I am troubled only by strange noises emanating from the lathe at certain speeds. My wife uses the sawdust and chips for mulching the gardens. Maybe this is why she gave me the lathe and saw. I must ask her about that.

A couple of weeks ago we started out for a look at your terrace, but the weather looked uncertain, so we settled for some pleasant wandering around Spruce Head and the Georges River. I hope you'll soon be walking on your terrace and defending it from invaders.

Yours,
Edmund W. Smith
Damariscotta, Maine

5 April 1957

Dear Mr. Smith:

Birds pose no problem for me, and I am an occasional visitor to Birdland, 1130 Fifth Avenue. Have just come from a sand spit on the Gulf Coast, where I saw a Great Blue Heron holding a rat in his beak and watched a catbird open up a hanging grapefruit. My problem is timing, and I don't want to take on any job, however pleasant, however easy to accomplish, lest it deflect me from the performance of my duty, which is to execute the commissions I have set for myself in this rugged vale. So I feel obliged to decline your kind invitation to write more bird captions, tempting though the prospect is.

As for the possibility of a book of the Harper designs, if he is anxious to go ahead with something of the sort, I don't want to be a hindrance, and he and you should get another caption writer and proceed. If anything of mine were made use of, an arrangement could be made, I would think; but I don't want to undertake to supply enough captions for a book.

Many thanks for your letter. I'm glad to have your progress report from your workshop in Damariscotta and I envy you your being in Maine at this time. I hope to come on soon but have not been feeling good and must await better omens.

Yrs.,
E. B. White

April 9, 1957

Dear Mr. White:

Of course I am sorry about your decision on the bird captions, but even your refusals are works of art, so I win anyway.

We're having a fine April blizzard today—about four inches already. It will soon be gone, and you will be coming to Maine, perhaps on that Bangor train, with boiled eggs and your thermos of coffee. May the cattails move rearward of the engine, and may you be feeling good health and spirits.

I'll keep you informed on any book developments, but I suspect it will be a couple more years before we get enough material gathered for a respectable volume.

High regards,
Edmund Ware Smith
Damariscotta, Maine

Damariscotta, Maine
November 25, 1957

Dear Mr. White:

I am again at large on the South Bristol Road after serving a ten-day stretch in Dearborn, during which my feet never touched sod or grass, only the chilled cement of railroad station platforms and the terrazzo floors of the Central Staff Office Building of the Ford Motor Company. While there my overall pain was added to by a touch of gout, which I consider a frightful injustice since for months I have subsisted on practically sub-marginal doses of gin and Coca Cola. However, it is possible the gout may have been in my head instead of my left big toe, since it began to subside soon after I boarded the Detroit-Boston sleeping car and opened the current issue of your magazine, in which, presently, I came upon your report with the November 12 Turtle Bay dateline.

Well, I see from your writings that my piece of beaver wood has made the *New Yorker*, thus bringing the Valley of the Wassataquoik—or New England's last wilderness—into the metropolis and creating an incidental nuisance in your apartment. I can picture you sitting on that sofa between the chip and the honorary hood. You were in damn good company.

With pride and delight, I showed your Turtle Bay piece to Jake Day* and Sawdust Hall, who accompanied me on the trip on which I procured the beaver chip which is causing all this trouble. When Jake and Sawdust came to the place where you stated your need for a beaver to eat the hood, they said—virtually in unison:

"By God! Let's send E. B. White a live beaver!"

Now, I can imagine how much you really want a live beaver, then or at present. But I, and I alone, have the powers of persuasion that can check the enthusiasm of Jake and Sawdust. I have never been in a better position to commit blackmail. You are in one hell of a spot, because you are the kind of man who can neither take a live beaver into your new abode, nor leave one alone if it showed up there.

So the deal is this: What with the fiftieth anniversary of the Model T coming up early in the new year, we are planning a special issue of the *Ford Times* in which, understandably, we would like to republish what is generally conceded to be the classic work on the Model T—"Farewell, My Lovely!" Will you please grant us permission to re-publish this piece for the price of $150, which, I believe, is what we paid for a previous re-printing around 1946? Or are you prepared to feed and care for a beaver? I would appreciate your early decision Mr. White, because if it is a negative we want to get up into the wilderness after the beaver before the freeze-up.

Seriously, I read "Farewell, My Lovely!" again while in the Dearborn office, and it's just as good as the day it was born. You may be assured it will be beautifully illustrated, if that means anything to you.

I hope this finds you well, and happily settled in your new residence, and I hope you are going to be in North Brooklin over Thanksgiving. It's fine here on the South Bristol Road, and my barn is loaded with dry maple firewood cut, split, and piled by me. Beautiful to burn and behold.

Please let me know about re-printing the story at the address below. I don't aim to be anywhere else but here for two months.

Kind regards,
Edmund Ware Smith
Damariscotta, Maine

P.S. I am embarrassed to say I'm not sure I have correctly remembered what we paid for the previous re-print privilege. Anyway, the price would be the same as for that. EWS

Jake Day is a reference to Damariscotta artist Maurice Day, illustrator of Disney's Bambi.

Thanksgiving 1957

Dear Mr. Smith:

I could have used a beaver very nicely a couple of weeks ago when I decided to recondition my pasture pond. It ended up by my using a backhoe at (I think) twenty dollars an hour. The pond, once a thing of beauty, now looks as though it had been gnawed by mastodons.

You may use the Model T piece in the *Ford Times* if it suits your fancy. I would appreciate it if you would split the check into two equal parts, making half to me and half to Richard L. Strout.* I will send you, in a day or two, the proper wording for the credit and for the copyright. I am too bushed at the moment to figure it out—on this piece it is a bit complicated on account of the co-authorship, and I will have to write to New York to find out how the copyright thing should be read.

Never try to remodel a back kitchen during the deer-hunting season. And if you have a flush toilet in your house, never allow it to backfire during November. I am sorry to hear that your barn is loaded with dry maple firewood. This should be in the woodshed. The cattle should be in the barn.

Yrs.,
E. B. White

*Send both to me and I will forward Strout one.

November 30, 1957
Last day of deer season

Dear Mr. White:

You are a good guy to take time out from the North Brooklin enterprises to write your consent for us to re-print "Farewell, My Lovely!"

I will see to it that separate checks are made out to you and Mr. Richard L. Strout, since I take pleasure in confusing the Central Staff Accounting Dept., which requires but small effort.

Our flush toilets (2) are working just fine, to date; but please do not mention pasture ponds or cattle again, because my wife, as a condition of our partnership, reads my mail. She has been hounding me for months for a pond and a cow, and had quieted down when your letter arrived. Now the whole thing has been reopened, and I am again reminding her that I am one of the few persons right around here who is able to milk a cow, and that if one is acquired I shall not go near it with stool or pail.

Hoping that you get rested, that your toilet is again working in the proper direction, and that your kitchen remodeling group will return to their task following the close of the deer season, I am, yours,

Sincerely,
Edmund Ware Smith

4 December 1957

Dear Smitty:

Why don't you, at this juncture, call me Whitey and I will call you Smitty? Then we can gradually adjust these tags as the years roll and the rockets mount.

My cows are the kind you don't have to milk—I saw to that. They are Herefords. In the spring each will drop a calf, one of them as a result of having an affair with a bull and the other as a result of a blind date with a man named Clifford Colby. These calves, when and if they appear, will take care of whatever milking has to be done. I don't know whether this news will exhilarate your wife or confound her. There was a milking stool on this place when I bought it, and it has been a great comfort to me. Nowadays the stool is always separated from a cow by a good safe distance.

Yrs.,
Whitey

December 6, 1957

Okay, Whitey, if that's the way you want it, but with the new tag, my vocabulary will change to Diversey Avenue and Delancey Street; and I was in them places once, too, see? Switch-Blade Smitty—that's I! When I was on the junk and looking for a fix, the pushers called me "Main-Line Mitty." So I been around, see?

The years are rolling all right, and so are the rockets mounting. What a hell of a long way we have come since the simple black powder burns and occasional resulting lockjaw of the Fourth of July of yesteryear—from the six-inch salute or cannon cracker to the subject of your interview with Fred at graveside in a recent *New Yorker*. No kidding, Whitey. That was a masterly if not supernal performance, both for you and the late animal. At the conclusion of the piece, I felt inspired, terrified, exhausted, and educated. Fred will live forever, and so, I hope, will his old man.

The mention of Fred brings up animals once again. In particular, it brings up cows, which, in my last letter, I asked you not to refer to again. What hath your disobedience wrought? It hath wrought—or may well wright—*three* cows. My wife asserts that she needs three of the beasts, because she has already named them: Smitty, Whitey, and Clifford Colby. I would that my tongue could udder the thoughts that arise in me.

I hope that Clifford Colby and the bull both did their work well and that, come spring, your kine will increase, your herd low and wind slowly o'er the lea.

Yours,
Smitty
Damariscotta, Maine

North Brooklin
1 January 1958

Dear Smitty:

Thank you for the Model T pictures; they are very fine and spirited, I think. I used one as part of a mantelpiece decoration along with spruce buds, china geese, and an old humidor. It worked out all right.

Very dark here today—just enough light in the sky to strike a match by. Best wishes for the New Year from

Yrs.,
Whitey

P.S. I hear you have set hours to write and transact business. I did that twenty years ago and they are still the laughing stock of Brooklin.

Sunday

January 12, 1958

Damariscotta, Maine

Dear Whitey:

Back to the South Bristol Road—and damn glad of it—after ten days battering in Dearborn. But our Model T issue, the dummy, that is, looks gorgeous. I just hope it goes through as dummied. I am pleased that one of the Model T pictures has a place in your mantelpiece decoration, along with the spruce buds, china geese, and the old humidor. But I am baffled by your postscript reference to my working hours. Whatever you heard is hearsay and not admitted in evidence. I have working hours, all right, but I do not necessarily do any work during them, and I enclose a photograph to prove it. The cat in my lap is named Sweet Life. Underneath the cat is a copy of *By Love Possessed*, which I was reading while supposedly working. The glass contains gin and Coke. Under it is *The Old Farmers' Almanac*, which I had been checking though for information on the lengthening of daylight following the winter solstice. The cigarette lighter doesn't work and seldom has. I try to fix it while working, and fail. It is a splendid instrument to aid procrastination, far superior to a nail file or pencil sharpener. Finally, take a look at those sheets of paper on my desk. Not a word on any of them, not even a trans-astral thumbprint. However, the chair I am sitting in was bought at Sloane's in New York, and it cost so much that I feel obliged to sit in it a certain number of hours every day. This may have started the rumor about my work schedule.

Yours,
Smitty

Tuesday, 1957

Dear Chief:

That's a fine snapshot of you at work. And it is a valuable reminder to me to carry my pyrabenzamine with me when I come to your place. I last about ten minutes in the same room with a cat, and then the asthma sets in and my tubes close. I have learned to carry cat pills, but sometimes forget them. I sincerely hope you get leprosy from dachshunds, so we can stay even-steven.

Yrs.,
Whitey

P.S. A pileated woodpecker stopped by here yesterday morning for about half an hour. I am enclosing a chip he threw down from a tree on our front lawn, where he was trying out a hole for size.

Thursday, Jan. 16, 1958

Dear Whitey:

I feel pretty bad about my cats and your asthma. If you'll just let me know a few hours in advance of your arrival, we'll get the cats off the premises and vacuum-clean the house. We have a new Hoover job, which is fun to operate and very effective in drawing cat hairs from rugs. And we would also lay in a good stock of pyrabenzamine, just in case. I am sorry to say that I don't get leprosy from dachshunds—just other lepers.

The token from your pileated woodpecker is joyously received. I have always admired the pileated, the drill press of the woods. I hope the hole in your tree fitted him and that he remains in residence.

How'd you like yesterday's northeaster? It was very fine, here, and put our new storm windows to the test. I worked hard throughout my entire schedule of hours for industry, reading the L.L. Bean and Farmall Tractor catalogs thoroughly. A good, productive day.

Highest regards to you and your dachshund.

Yours,
Smitty
Damariscotta, Maine

March 14, 1957

Dear Whitey:

The end is near. Yesterday morning, on the upper reaches of the South Bristol Road, I saw maple trees being tapped. The sap buckets were Gulf Pride oil cans. *Sacre du printempts* my eye! I'd sooner see a plastic pussy willow or a paper crocus.

My wife and I read what you and your wife wrote in your magazine recently, and were pleased and enlightened. It is fine to know you are there in North Brooklin procrastinating and enjoying the Whitefaces (cows) and the byre. I am doing likewise, except that instead of Whitefaces I am enjoying the creation of a room in my barn for the display of my wife's vegetables.

We have purchased a Rototiller, and I dread the moment of its arrival. We also purchased the new *Encyclopedia Britannica*, and now that it is here and installed I can't think of a thing to look up. I know everything—except why people use Gulf Pride oil cans for sap buckets.

Yours in anguish,
Smitty
Damariscotta, Maine

The Lowell
Friday, March 1958

Dear Smitty:

Your letter reached me when I was in the hospital with pneumonia. I got sick in Maine and then I came to New York for a few days and got sicker. We had Bedroom A from Bangor, and my only recollection of Bedroom A is climbing down the ladder at 2 a.m. with a fever of 102 in order to get an aspirin tablet and a split of White Rock, the location of which I knew. When I finally made it back upstairs, I discovered that I had not remembered the opener. So I had to make the trip all over again.

I was pretty sure that if I made the ridiculous mistake of leaving home in March, one of my white-faced heifers would choose that time to drop her calf, and that is exactly what happened. She went down into the woods before daylight last Sunday morning, with the snow quite deep (I am told), and had a snowdrop. The fellow that works for me found the group at 6 a.m., went back to the barn for a sled, and dragged the calf up for its first drink of colestrum and bourbon. (I have no dictionary in this hotel and that word for first milk looks all wrong.) I sympathize with you with that Rototiller. You should have bought a Farmall Cub tractor, the most versatile machine since the Model T. Speaking of Fords, you might like to read a piece I wrote on automobile design while running a fever in the pavilion last week. I think it will appear next week in the *NYer* under the title "Letter from the North." My stepson has been trying to give me your *Maine Treasury*, for my convalescence, but met reverses. However, he is working on it.

I have a grandson who has been sugaring, and for all I know he used Gulf Pride. I can still remember vividly the sap operations of my son, about twenty years ago, when our kitchen was the scene of a really fine brand of turmoil.

Your wife is an optimist, my wife says. (I refer to that order blank.)

Yrs.,
Whitey

P.S. What's the matter with Gulf Pride? You're just an old romanticist, dreaming of wooden sap buckets. Besides, the maples on my place are not sugar maples at all, and they need a dash of cylinder oil to tone up the sap.

April 4, 1958

Damariscotta, Maine

Dear Whitey:

My initial reaction to "Letter From the North" is glee of the more vengeful sort. If your decision against buying a new machine starts a human movement in that direction, the stylists will get what I have long thought they deserve. My more studied reaction to the piece was that it was in too low a key. Maybe this was intentional to give a sobering effect, but I found myself wishing for diatribe and vituperation. I am going to be in Detroit next Thursday, and will doubtless gather a lot of reactions to "Letter from the North" from the source. If I get anything good, I'll let you know. Incidentally, my machine is a 1955 Ranch Wagon and will remain so for some time, or maybe longer, now that I have read and approved L from the N. No kidding, I have wondered if and when the stylists were going to perish from self-imitation, the most insidious form of inbreeding.

I sympathize with your ladder work in Bedroom A, and am very glad to hear your pneumonia is a thing of the past, but drinking White Rock at 2 a.m. is something I would suspect of a Detroit stylist.

How much is the new calf? Certainly its initial potion of bourbon-milk punch puts it a cut above its owner in the drinking field. Notes from "Walpole Gardens" are not near as thrilling. I have built several miles of tomato fence, and picked a cirque of rocks from the land so they won't ruin the new Rototiller. When you buy a new car, and thus start the automobile industry booming again so I can make some dough, we'll trade the tiller for a Farmall Cub, which was what we wanted all along.

"Old romanticist dreaming of wooden sap buckets" is right. That's me—especially since I see where they are tapping the trees with a plastic hose arrangement, like a milking machine.

That's pretty nice about your stepson trying to give you *A Treasury of the Maine Woods*. It was chosen as the January Kit Book for the U.S. Armed Forces, so there was a shortage and a second printing, which has just recently been circulated. I was irritated by the publisher, who insisted on calling it a treasury. There are so many "treasuries" plopping off the presses that the word has lost even its ostentation. I didn't see how you have a Maine treasury anyway, without something by Thoreau or Sarah Orne Jewett, so I suggested to the publisher that we call it a "Sub-Treasury." He didn't even laugh, so I gave in, and now he is claiming the title accounts for the book's success. Maybe he's right, at that.

I'm sending this to North Brooklin hoping you're there and in good health again. My wife admits to your wife that she (my wife) is an optimist.

Yours,
Smitty
Damariscotta, Maine

Tuesday, April 15, 1958
Dearborn, Mich.

Dear Whitey:

Most of the boys in the Publications Department (Department C7-1 to you) are in agreement with "Letter From the North"—in particular our talented Art Director, who is downright enthusiastic. I haven't dared venture into the Styling Department for its reaction. I don't know anyone there I could trust, and I am too young for the guillotine.

We took great pleasure yesterday in scheduling the October issue of *Ford Times*, which leads off with "Farewell, My Lovely!" We expect to subtitle it, "The greatest piece of prose ever written about an automobile," or something equally imposing.

I now come to the tragic part of my report. There is a strong, insistent rumor throughout these halls that the DeSoto automobile is to be discontinued. No kidding.

Well, you've still got the '49, so what the hell.

I am homeward bound tonight, so the remaining hours of this day will be stubborn. Yours for the land of the pointed firs and cat spruce,

Smitty

North Brooklin
Monday

Dear Smitty:

What I need is a beaver that can strain the clay particles out of pond water, by breathing in and out. If you know of a beaver equipped for that sort of work, let me know about him.

The way to visit us here is to watch the weather, pick a good chance, and start driving. But it would be a good idea to signal me by phone or by postcard, to make sure I will be on hand. The only day I don't relish visitors is Sunday, when I devote myself exclusively to needy animals, dirty garbage pails, and empty wood boxes. We would like you to come over in time for lunch, or better yet, come over in the afternoon and stay the night, and we will kick you out the next morning after breakfast. If your wife can leave that dreadful little machine long enough to accompany you, we would love to have her. Some of the ice has melted along the terrace, and we can probably sit out there if we bundle up good and take plenty to drink.

This has been a weird spring. Last week we had a Harris's sparrow with us for several days. I had never seen one before, and my books say they seldom get east of the Alleghenies. One of my heifers is due to freshen this week, and if the calf comes while you are visiting, you'll just have to shift for yourself. If you stay the night, you will be in a good position to see the coon. She has kittens in the tree, and appears about 8:10 p.m.

To get me by phone, ask for Sedgwick, Maine, and the number is ELgin 9-8341. Name is

Whitey

May 30, 1958

Dear Whitey:

I will watch the weather, and some day next week, on a good report on the six p.m. broadcast, I will call that ELgin number, make a date for lunch the next day, and start driving. My wife states that she would leave that dreadful engine of hers for no other purpose whatever—but can't stand to be away from it overnight, which means we'll have to miss the coon, hangover and all.

No Harris sparrow has checked in here, but there's a Bobolink on the lawn right now.

My beavers, unfortunately, are not the clay particle-straining type, but your farm pond problem is receiving a good deal of attention here. My good friend Edward Myers (although Princeton) reports that he has communicated with you about the same kind of gypsum treatment. By great good fortune, it happens that my nephew, Alfred Eipper, is head of the New York State farm pond department, or bureau, and has published several heady papers on the subject. We'll bring these documents when we head for your terrace, where we can discuss clay academically. My nephew got his doctor's degree from your alma mater, so he must be hot stuff.

On my recent trip to the Katahdin region, I visited with an old friend of mine who was at Cornell with you. He is Hans Huber, and seems to wear his several hundred producing oil wells gracefully.

I think your wife's catalog story caused more excitement in gardening circles than yours on styling did among the automobile people. Several local fans have triumphantly named catalogs—

erudite ones, I gather—that weren't mentioned. I'll bet your wife has heard all about it by this time! We can put this subject on the agenda for the terrace, which I look forward to being on.

Yours,
Smitty
Damariscotta, Maine

June 7, 1958

Dear Whitey and Katharine:

Our feeling—after several days' afterglow—is that your price of a million bucks for the terrace is about right. You may have underestimated a little since you had no way of anticipating a minister of the gospel in full sight—what I would call a working lay preacher, as we viewed him tooling down the aisles of your fine, but retarded, vegetable garden.

Driving home (we took Route 90 through Warren as per your hint and saved much time), we were worried about the coon, the goslings, the minister, and, above all, Ellsworth.* Your invitation to the accouchement sounded sincere. We thought of turning back, but figured you and Ellsworth would want to be alone during this crisis, and I might have made some remark that would have interrupted the smooth, supremely private agony of a mother producing a child.

Mary and I think your home is beautiful. We were teed off by the relationship between you and Mrs. Tainter, and the other people there in the garden, on the soil, in the house. It's one of those places where nobody hates anybody, and it fulfills all of our anticipation of both of you through all our ridiculous correspondence through all these years, and all the things we have read that you both have written in the public prints.

We must make a return engagement before Andy departs for the haying season. We want you to see our Rototiller work. But perhaps even more than that, I want to make a date with Katharine some Tuesday—her day off—to go down to Deerfield to Frank Boyden's silent laboratory and break up by night a few Erlenmeyer Flasks.

Our affection, admiration, and obligation to you, Ellsworth, her possible young Fryburg, August-the-leper, and the geese, ganders, goslings, and Whites, one and all.

Please tell your gardener that this is gospel.

Smitty and Mary

A cow.

N. Brooklin
11 June 1958

Dear Smitty:

You should have stuck around. My Cow Ellsworth had a fine heifer calf at 4:30 that afternoon, after only an hour of horsing around. The calf is a deep chocolate brown, with a white star on its forehead. Ellsworth gave a nice performance and would have gladly disemboweled anybody who so much as glanced sideways at her delicious chocolate drop. Art Waldron dropped in later to pick up his raccoon and was surprised that my new calf was wet. He wanted to know whether that was because its mother had been licking it. So I ended the day explaining the facts of life to Art Waldron.

There is no parson here today and things are quiet. The vegetable garden looks less like a proving ground for non-atomic weapons than it did the day you were here. We leave for New York on Monday, to test the pollen count on East 63rd Street.

Yrs,
Andy

August 28, 1958

Dear Whitey:

Those frightened little people did it to us—a lot to me, but most to you. The sons of bitches changed son of a bitch to son of a gun in your story: and they are scared of what they did to both of us, as the enclosed explanation will indicate. The letter is from Jerome Palms, a very nice associate editor and production man, who doesn't swear hardly at all, and is a Catholic boy with six children.

Well, anyway, as Jerry Palms remarks, the story looks nice in the book and probably only a few of us hard shells will miss the son of a bitch. What hurts me is, it just isn't son of a gun what the man said. Mercy on us, and my gracious!

How was the pollen count on East 62nd? Are you home? And how is Ellsworth's calf that we missed seeing born?

The report from Walpole Gardens is financially and aesthetically excellent. But we confess looking forward to Labor Day, when the Jaguars, Cadillacs, and various station wagons go south with their loads of vacationers and antiques and leave us the hell alone.

Wait two days after you read here what happened to the words from the mouth of the ferry boat captain. Then write me a reply, if you've cooled off enough by that time.

Yours, in anguish,
Smitty
Damariscotta, Maine

North Brooklin
31 August 1958

Dear Smitty

Don't worry about the ferry boat captain; he has been remodeled before, and I am used to it by now. I feel merely a mild sadness, no anger. It is a little unsettling to realize that many people don't want to read an exact report of an incident, they want it reported as seen through the distorting mirror of their own likes and dislikes. Anyway, what the man said was, "Let's pull the son of a bitch up onto the boat." I remember it so clearly, even though it was so long ago. Probably if he had said son of a gun, I would never have thought of it again.

The old piece certainly looks fine in its new presentation with the James Warren paintings. When I was in New York in June I had lunch with my old sidekick, Howard Cushman, who made the trip with me in the T.

My attempt to escape hay fever by going to New York was farcical. The season was about three weeks late, as I should have known, and I arrived back with haying in full swing—if you can call what we did here this summer haying. It was more like sponge diving most of the time. Ellsworth's calf is lusty and handsome, and will probably remain so if I can get around to cutting out the chokecherry along the fence lines before the first killing frost. I'm glad the Walpole Gardens had a good season and hope you own a nice light clam hoe for the potato-digging days. Our freezer is loaded with berries and vegetables, and all we need is a hurricane to knock the power out for three days. Am fattening my young geese on wormy apples (as though I grow any other kind), and if you know of any child who would like some Buff

Cochin bantam chicks, let me know—I raised them as painlessly as I do barn swallows, which they sometimes resemble.

Two carloads of children and grandchildren have pulled out of here, one yesterday morning, one this morning, bound back to work and school, and we have a strong end-of-summer feeling. The Blue Hill Fair is in full swing, but hasn't enjoyed my custom yet.

Yrs,
Whitey

17 January 1959

Dear Smitty:

I think this exchange is all right, now; I was chiefly against it at first because the letters contained my name and address and were an invitation to writer-hunters to get out their roadmaps.

The textbook is one I used almost forty years ago, by the late William Strunk, Jr., and Macmillan is planning to reissue it this spring, with a preface and a chapter on writing by me. It has been a headache for many months, because they wanted me to revise the text and I don't know anything about rhetoric. Title: *The Elements of Style*. I will send you a copy if you send me a copy of *For Maine Only*.

Yrs,
Andy

June 3, 1959

Dear Whitey:

I have been a long time acknowledging Strunk & White on *The Elements of Style*. It made me try to write sentences with no words, which is why you haven't heard from me before now. It's a fine book, and I am delighted and enlightened. "Cogent" is a word which comes to mind, but I am still a little scared of the shade of Will Strunk, Jr.

My son Jim, whom I recently visited in Bishop, Calif., introduced me to mountain driving in the High Sierras, scaring me out of my wits. There were moments on Sabrina Lake Road when I would have paid handsomely for one look at a pool table or any flat surface that I couldn't fall off of. But the trip was worth it, just to see the boy fully matured, confident, and happily at home in a community of his own choice. My two grandsons, seven and three, are both geologists. They collect rocks, many of which I stepped on while walking around their house.

Jim met me at the Reno airport for the drive southward over the mountains to Bishop; but before starting the auto trip, I decided to eat a hamburger. It cost me seventy bucks because in the hamburger joint there were gaming tables.

"Pop," said Jim, nudging me away from the green cloth, "you better stay away from blackjack till you can add up to twenty-one."

He then paused a few minutes at a crap table and won eight or nine pounds of silver dollars. The drive to Bishop proceeded with spirits high, with the once-small boy I taught the rudiments of poker at the wheel. I don't know whether I was scareder driving over those mountains, or flying over them at 20,000 ft. altitude, the fancy word for droppage. But the South Bristol Road looked good to me when I reached it.

About our book-trade agreement, my work is slated to appear in August. I was going to write you that I had been stuck on the deal, because my book costs $3.95, while yours goes for $2.50. But I see now where I win out in meat content. Very high protein in *Elements of Style*. The adjective is allowable in this instance.

Any chance that you and Katharine would drive over here some good day for lunch and look at our garden? That's if we got the cats off the premises. Tel. Damariscotta LOcust 3-3959

Thanks again for the book.

Yours,
Smitty
Damariscotta, Maine

North Brooklin
21 June 1959

Dear Smitty:

Thanks for your letter and the copy of your critical remarks on our carnality fellows. I am in agreement with your sentiments, my only trouble being I am always so far behind in my reading. Haven't caught up with *L. Chatterly's Lover* yet, which puts me easily thirty-five years behind. And I must get to work and read *Lolita*. Started it a year ago and it failed to hold my interest. A writer who does hold my interest is the author of *The Harmless People*—a book about the Bushman. I recommend it.

Our house for the next few weeks will crawl with grandchildren. Joe and his wife are expecting their third by Caesarean section next Wednesday, and we are taking his other two youngsters here, also our oldest grandchild, Kitty Stableford, who will study French in the morning, babysit in the afternoon, and wonder whether she can have the car in the evening.

The nine days' rain appears at this writing to be over, but I won't believe this blue sky till I see more of it. Yesterday I strained my back lifting a case of liquor (we feed our grandchildren neat gin), and today I cannot lift a 10-quart pail of water for the hens and it is all I can do to lift a highball glass for myself. Shot a porcupine last night; he was high up in a locust tree, eating his way down. We have several big locusts on the place, but the porkies have killed three.

In your Thoreau piece in the March issue of the *Ford Times* you said that the village of Shin Pond has excellent tourist accommodations. Can you name one for my information? I just might drive up there some day this summer to have a look round, as I have never been in that part of the state.

Speaking of carnality, which you (not I) brought up, did you ever read the novel (can't think of title or author's name) in which the hero and a nature-girl dove into a beaver pond, eluding pursuers, and surfaced *inside* the beaver house. There they found love. It is my favorite American setting (to date) for coupling. Must be a cinch to write a novel—you just think up a beaver house and work backwards from there.

Yrs,
Whitey

North Brooklin
25 (I think) August 1959

Dear Smitty:

Instead of making it to Shin Pond, I made it to Harkness Pavilion, where I laid up for nine days while they played many a merry trick on me. I think the gayest of all was the day I got back to my room after a long, gaudy session in x-ray where they watched the play-by-play in my lower bowel. Exhausted, I crawled into my bed and lay there breathing and dying. Two minutes later, a nurse popped in, and said in a cheery voice: "Mr. White? We've come for your bed." They had, too. The nurse and an orderly rolled it out of the room, leaving me sitting on a hassock, and were gone for forty-five minutes. It seems they needed a bed somewhere, and picked mine as the one that would be least rumpled. (I always keep my drawsheet nice and tight.)

I heard about your Orono appearance from a Bangor friend who attended. Orono will be a healthier place when they discover liquor. I've had two sessions there (during which I had the decency to keep my trap shut), and both of them stand out brilliantly in memory as being parched and dry. When I get dry enough, I shake all over.

The Elements of S. is now on the bestseller list, and this indicates something ominous in our society, as worrisome as fallout. In one bookshop below 14th Street, Strunk is outselling *Lady Chatterley's Lover*. It's a topsy-turvy world, and I can't help being alarmed.

Have you been reading about the beavers who keep plugging up a culvert under a highway in Hampden? The wardens have been blasting them with everything in the book, but they still come back and lay a few sticks across the culvert, flooding the tar. If I get time I'm going over. But I never get time.

Yrs.,
Andy

P.S. My constitution is OK. I just had a gut ache that lasted six weeks. Usually mine last only five, so I was alarmed.

Any minute now I expect to look up and see a yawl in the cove, with Steven Rockefeller and Anne Marie aboard. They will want to use the telephone, to call the Rasmussens in Soegne. Steven will forget to leave the money.

September 22, 1959

Dear Whitey:

I am glad to learn from yours of the 22nd of August that you survived having your bed pulled out from under you at the Pavilion and that your organs are okay. You may get to Shin Pond yet, and earliest October is likely to be a good time, although Thoreau made his trip down the East Branch in August. There were black flies. He called fly dope "insect wash." He also called a canoe's thwart a "crossbar."

Elements of Style continues to adorn the bestseller lists. I follow it in *Time* magazine, and it seems to be teetering on the tight wire in the neighborhood of *The Years with Ross* and *How I Turned $1000 into $1,000,000 in Real Estate*. I am not the man to draw any conclusions, especially after your information about Strunk & White status on *Lady Chatterly's Lover*. What disturbs me is that there must be a lot of people trying to learn about style. That means more writers, more competition, a harder struggle for me, and perhaps you. Watch it, will you, Whitey?

For Maine Only was mailed to you today. It is a runaway bestseller in Damariscotta—eight copies to date have been purchased, three of them by me. "The Outermost Henhouse" chapter, in which a couple of your letters appear anonymously, didn't fool a sharp Radcliffe senior friend of ours.

"Who wrote the letters?" she asked.

"The man wishes to remain unidentified," I said.

"Hah! It's E. B. White. You can't fool me."

"I'm not trying to fool you," I said. "*He* is."

Were you in the lobby of the Lafayette Hotel in Portland last Saturday morning about nine a.m.? My wife says she saw you, or your twin. She had driven down to meet me on my return from

Detroit where I had been for a week indoctrinating the *Ford Times* editorial staff with the elements of style. They are better men for my visit, and I am slightly richer and a lot tireder.

What with recent frosts, the garden project is about about to wind up for the season. It was successful and well done; now I can turn the full fire of my creative effort to my workshop each afternoon. I am making a four-poster canopy bed for a lady. Already I have one leg turned.

Never got to see the Hampden beaver, but some ghoul ran over a huge one just below us on the So. Bristol Road ten days ago.

Yours sincerely,
Smitty
Damariscotta, Maine

North Brooklin
15 October 1959

Dear Smitty:

I was out behind the barn yesterday watching Prin Allen push
his jack knife through a 10 × 10 sill, and I heard a noun I
thought you ought to know about. Prin said he had gone down
to the Point to see Gene Holden about putting a thrush hole in
his kitchen doorway. I'll bet that crazy place of yours in Damariscotta hasn't got a thrush hole in the doorway.

I've been enjoying *For Maine Only* and will like it better when
I can read it in health, as I have been poorly. Just as soon as one
section of my body gets through bedeviling me, another section
grabs the baton and is off and away. I liked that Doctor in *Privilege* who talked about himself in the third person, and I like the
doing away of Rip Skillinger's dog. For a long time I had a friend
who walked like Zeb Trunk, lifting his feet (which never toed in
or out) and setting them down carefully. His name was Robert
Weston, and one Saturday he just walked out to an abandoned
rifle range and shot himself in sorrow.

I don't know what you were doing in Dahlonega, but I guess
it's none of my business. Probably you walked all the way down
there on that trail. Your chapter on Poland Spring makes me
eager to put in an order at the store for a case of Hiram Ricker's
pure brew in the green bottles. My father always ordered a bottle of Poland water when he rode the train or sat in a summer
hotel dining room. It gave the occasion class, and I still think I
should introduce a little class around here. I reread "Outermost
Henhouse" and was struck all over again by an odd piece of
nature faking in there, unless you can submit an affidavit. Have
you, Edward Smith, ever seen a robin's nest lined with white

feathers? Robins used to use horse hair for a liner, when there were horses around, and they use dry grass, string, cloth, and sundry fibrous materials. I've never seen a nest with a feather lining but I am only a fair-weather observer. Barn swallows are the birds to whom a white feather means everything. They finish up their nest with a white feather the way a young modern finishes up his split-level ranch house with a fancy aluminum grille on the front door, just over the thrush hole. Did I ever tell you my theory about the white feather in a barn swallow's nest. (You can't stop me even if I did.) My theory is that this white feather is a beacon, guiding the bird straight home in the dark shadowy barn when swooping through the doorway out of the bright sunlight. That sentence has no grammar to speak of, but the theory may stand up anyway.

Hope you are well and that your book continues to run away in the shops. Having put a book about semicolons on the non-fiction list, I feel that my work is done, and I can now just curl up with a bottle of Poland water and let the world go by. Katharine, on the other hand, still thinks of the future. She is out this morning after a hard frost, opening little holes in the border for bulbs. The 10 × 10 sill I told you about earlier is to hold up two bantam hens and a rooster. Combined weight approx. 4½ lbs. I never got to Shin Pond or anywhere else, but thanks for the directions. Fix your doorway.

Yrs,
Whitey

November 4, 1959

Dear Whitey:

I see by this weeks' *Time* where *Elements of Style* has pushed its way above *This Is My God*, and I approve of this evidence of strength. I would have answered yours of the 15th of October sooner, but was recovering from four days on and around Katahdin with Justice Douglas, an experience I can recommend only for the fearless, the bottomless, and men of stout arches. I was nearly suffocated with enlightenment, Jack Daniels, and fresh air.

Mr. Holdren's noun, thrush hole, is a beautiful word, and I think of it every time I step over one. Before long, in response to your accusation of nature faking, you will receive a robin's nest lined with white feathers, thus proving that a bird which can make the transition from horse hair to string, grass, and cloth, can go on from there. Your theory on the barn swallow's use of white feather is sound, to my way of thinking. I will take it up with some of the Audubon boys, giving you full credit.

If you want to know, I was in Dahlonega writing a piece for the *Ford Times*. I have been a lot of places writing pieces for the *Ford Times*. I went to all of the places after I had learned to hate traveling, too. Think of the younger men who would have loved it. On the other hand, the hell with them.

I hope the 10 × 10 sill is supporting the bantams okay. More than that, I hope you have recovered from the ailments which seemed to be responsible for a note of melancholy in your letter. Katharine's thinking of the future is right-minded. When doom threatens, buy a new suit of clothes and some gin, a twenty years' supply.

Or drive over here and see the nearly completed four-poster I am finishing up in time for Christmas delivery to Edward Myers' daughter, Felicity. It's built to last forever, since Felicity is only four years old.

Yours,
Smitty
Damariscotta, Maine

Tuesday, Dec. 29, 1959

Dear Smitty:

Am confined to bed with a bad case of Noel, with accompanying sore throat, also an accompanying N.E. blizzard, so please excuse pencil scrawl. The robin you sent me is a sensation—a beautiful bird in all respects. I immediately removed him from that phony nest, took a real robin's nest from one of my apple trees, installed the nest right beside the kitchen porch steps where we have a temporary fir balsam, and placed the robin in the nest, and he has delighted all who come and go. Did you carve him yourself? I hope so. The nest with the white feathers is also a fine piece of mimicry and shows to what lengths a man will go to restore himself, once having fallen into error. It belongs peculiarly to the year 1959, I feel—the year of widespread chicanery. I love to think of the hours you and Mary must have given to the falsification of the nest, with you plundering all the old barns in the neighborhood for the white feathers, and Mary standing ready with the tube of Duco cement as you dashed home with the latest trophy. I haven't taken this matter up with the Audubon people yet or with Justice Douglas, as I have been too busy and too sick; but I am preserving the nest carefully on the workbench in my shop, until such time as I can introduce it in evidence and get the world's opinion of it. (In the spring I plan to show it to a robin.)

Hope you are both well and happy and enjoying the storm more than I am today. I like storms when I can meet them with my pants on, but am less fond of them when they catch me in pajamas. You added greatly to the gaiety of my Christmas, you and that bird.

Yrs.,
Whitey

December 31, 1959

Dear Whitey:

That was a hell of a fine northeaster, depositing 13.6" here-abouts—nothing to challenge in my jamas. While it was building up, Joe French and Moose Millward came down in their truck and installed a new Schoolhouse Stove for heating my barn work-shop. Some stove! Everything but a sandbox for spitting. I spent most of the day lighting fires in it and listening to its expansion noises. Its pipe and draft in a gale are better than bagpipes.

That robin, far from being carved by me, was the creation of Dorothy Washington. She is a director of the Audubon Society, and she once rented a Cambridge apartment to your son Joel. We pick only the best people for our robin work. She is one of your devoted followers and took on our assignment with zest.

The nest, before it got feathered, was the work of a robin who bivouacked in our box elder last spring. I poked it off a high limb with a canoe pole, catching it as it fell. The green grass growing from its mud walls was nature's work. We had to have White Rock feathers, because our birds in the O. Henhouse were White Rocks, and this had to be an authentic phony. The only White Rock owner we knew was Larry Day, former manager of the Bethel Inn, currently doing post office work and chicken raising. Larry supplied us with White Rock feathers, the donors being a couple of birds named Sarah and Laura. Given feathers and a pot of adhesive, Mary did the rest. The enterprise was enjoyed by one and all, possibly excepting Sarah and Laura. We like to think of the robin in its new nest in the fir balsam beside your kitchen porch steps.

I used to think you were pretty snooty having a minister in to weed your garden. You want to know who plows my driveway

after snowstorms? One man, who drives the big plow, is named
Oliver Wendell Holmes. The second man, who drives the jeep
plow, really getting into the corners, is Gordon Merriam, former
ambassador to Egypt and Israel.

We survived Christmas okay, but I am dubious about a New
Year's party we are attending tonight at Ed Myers'. So I am getting this letter off to you before anything happens to me. Happy
New Year to you and Katharine, and hoping that you've got your
pants on again, I am yours truly,

Smitty
Damariscotta, Maine.

Sarasota

January 13, 1960

Dear Smitty:

I have some castoff clover hay I'm going to give away; in case you know anybody wants it they can just step across my thrush hole and it's theirs.

Whitey

On a postcard of the Yarmouth–Bar Harbor Ferry.

February 4, 1960

Dear Whitey:

I was going to write you all about my sore back and the amount of distress it caused me on my recent Dearborn trip, when a much happier subject turned up in the *New York Times* of February 2nd. Our friend Edward Myers (I made the four-poster canopy bed for his daughter, Felicity) brought the clipping in last evening, and the picture on the left, which looks like Cesar Romero, is captioned E. B. White. I am glad it's really you, and that Glenway Wescott announced the gold medal award. He was some punkins as a novelist around the early thirties, if I remember good. Your running mate, Charles Burchfield, was recently done in watercolor for the *Ford Times*, and it is a fine thing to see two *Ford Times* contributors side-by-side in splendor. Enthusiastic congratulations to you.

A lesser, but very disturbing honor has just been conferred, or dropped—like an anvil—on me. I have been made editorial director of the *Ford Times*. In a backhanded way, you and Charles Burchfield may be partly responsible. You get guys like White & Burchfield in your magazine, and the authorities have to do something with you. I am not sure I am going to like what they did. It means one week per month in Dearborn instead of one week in two months. I may be creeping into the rat race I have devoted a lifetime to avoiding—a hell of a situation to get into at almost sixty years of age. I have promised my benefactors to give it a whirl for six months.

My wife is convinced that she can see evidences of spring in the slenderer maple and willow limbs. I say it is an illusion created by the change in light, as the days lengthen. It's been a swell winter here, so far, and no yearnings at this writing for Florida.

Dorothy Washington, the great lady who fashioned your robin, wanted me to warn you that the bird's colors—or paint job—are not for outdoor living. If the colors have run, or washed off, due to exposure, she says she will gladly re-do them for you.

Will you have to make a speech in May when receiving that gold medal? Or will they just send it along to North Brooklin, insured for a million bucks? In my dreams of winning Pulitzers or Nobels, I always drop them a postcard saying: "Please send check."

Yours,
Smitty
Damariscotta, Maine

February 8, 1960

Dear Smitty:

Cesar Romero is the name I used when I was in the pictures—it is what they call a non de plume—(I did not like to use my real name) and was only an actor because it gives an opportunity to kiss girls, which is "all to the good."

If you have back trouble, go to the Institute for the Crippled and Disabled, and get fitted for a corset. I did this, against my will, and have no regrets. I have thrown my back out in a number of different ways, many of them bizarre, but I have managed always to get it back in place again thanks to the artistry of the Institute. They never gave me a gold medal. But if your back feels good you don't need one.

Dorothy Washington's robin is under cover, in a nest a robin built halfway down the stairs to the barn cellar. It is slightly faded, but so is a nesting robin.

Yrs.,
Whitey

P.S. Congratulations on your appointment as editorial director, but watch out. The cities always put up a big fight when they find one of their boys has defected. The cities can't take it, and they keep fighting back.

July 2, 1960

Dear Smitty:

Thanks for sending me your piece on my favorite Justice and the Thoreau pieces. I have enjoyed both.

Have been in poor health so not communicative. They keep taking pictures of my guts, and I feel overexposed and dispirited.

It's OK to use whatever you want from the *Ford Times*. I don't recall writing anything about the whip-poor-will but maybe I did. Am at the moment observing at close range a pair of redstarts working themselves to the bone to launch one cowbird nestling. The nest is a handsome little structure in a lilac bush just outside my study window. The young cowbird hatched several days in advance of the only redstart to hatch, and the nest now consists of one large lusty cowbird, one dead redstart nestling, and two long-gone eggs, which the female still tries to incubate, against all possible odds. Here in this tiny family circle we see the triumph of promiscuity and irresponsibility over fidelity and zeal. The world will be richer by one cowbird when all is over, and I have been tempted to step outside my door and mix in, in an attempt to restore justice, but have resisted. The little redstart hen allows me to approach within two feet. Only an angry God would permit cowbirds to take such an unfair advantage, but I am reconciled to having God mad more than half the time, as indeed I am, too.

Yrs.,
Whitey

July 29, 1960

Dear Whitey:

Your letter of July 2 about the redstart-cowbird trouble outside your study window pulled a lot of us together and caused us to feel less sorry for self. It is a crime that a guy who sends out shafts of light through the mail, as you do, should have to suffer from long-term bellyaches and ailments of the flesh, and photography of the same to boot. No wonder you and God are mad half the time.

I was thinking of you night before last coming from New York to Portland on the *State of Maine* because I was on a train. I had recently been on several airplanes to and from Detroit and was looking forward to a trip where I could forget the law of gravity for a while, but I think the engineer of the *State of Maine* was trying to commit suicide. He made up twenty-five minutes of time in the last hour-and-a-half or so, bringing the train into Portland only five minutes behind schedule. I was shook up. I felt like the kitten I once put on the turn-table of a Victrola many years ago. Served me right.

What you wrote about the Whip-poor-Will is this:

"Marked like a toad, mustached like a walrus, behaving like an owl, this repetitious bird comes to one's doorstone before daylight to unhinge the mind. What does 'Whip poor Will' mean? Nothing. Who is Will? Nobody knows. If nature were evil, this moon-bird would be her favorite child. Yet heard at a little distance, its message is one of the sweetest in the orchestra of night."

Such was the bird who "unhinged our minds" from its perch—not on our doorstone, but on our tent rope one night during Justice Douglas's last trip. So I thought your description would go good in my story of the scene.

I thought of you again on this last Detroit trip, not because I was on a train, but because I saw an ad in a magazine displaying a device for purifying the air in a room, ridding it of all pollens and irritating stuff. I wondered if you had come across the device, and if it would make life better for you during haying season?

One more item: What is the address of that place where you get corsets for lame backs? I think I'm going to have to get one, if you will tell me where.

Yours,
Smitty
Damariscotta

North Brooklin
2 August 1960

Dear Smitty

Sorry to hear that your back has turned up. I am enclosing the address of the Institute for the Crippled and Dejected.

I'm not sure you should plunge into a corset unless you have a doctor's signal. My corset was prescribed for me by one of the New York clowns, and I had to show up at the Institute for a fitting. The garment is as carefully built as a boat, and I doubt that it would do any good if it were not. You describe your back as "lame" and this may be a muscular problem. My back is (like the rest of me) slightly deranged, that is, there is a minor foul-up among a couple of the lower vertebrae. Most of the time I'm fine—can lift and heave up to a decent point. But a slight twist, or lifting while at a disadvantage, can throw me out of line. I did this about ten days ago merely by turning and looking back while at the wheel of a pickup truck—(I was trying to see whether my granddaughter was still in place in the rear of the vehicle). I went right into my corset, wearing it for only two or three hours a day, and am now in line again. It is a fabulous garment, but you have to have the right thing wrong with you. So you better damn well find out, if you don't already know for sure.

Katharine is the veteran of the war of the back. About twelve years ago she was all washed up—could not stand or sit or lie without bad pain. She took this problem to Dr. Frank Stinchfield, who is the head bone man at the Columbia-Presbyterian, and he took her apart and put her together again with excellent results. I can recommend this guy without any reservation in case you are in serious difficulty. He had a great experience in the war, patching up busted human beings, and he is an extremely likable medico. Offhand, I would say that if your back is suffering from tired muscles (too much Douglas on the Mount) you need some horse liniment, but if your back is badly aligned or contains a vertebra that is crumbling, then you need a corset. And that is all today from old Doctor White. By the way, do you wear sneakers or moccasins a great deal of the time? That can do it to me.

If you were only "shook up" by a ride on the *State of Maine*, you are doing all right. One of the engineers has a little nephew about ten years old who rides with him and occasionally handles the controls, and while this child was at the throttle one time, I happened to be in the toilet room, or "annex," shaving. The little tike's hand slipped off the throttle, just as we were coming into Old Orchard, and hit the air brake lever. I was not ready. I came out of the annex backwards and fetched up against a pile of news magazines in the lower berth, raking one elbow and narrowly missing the steel bottom of the upper berth with my head. I received a solicitous letter from the railroad, as did every passenger on the train—all six of us. I never did get the kid's autograph.

Thanks for reminding me of the whip-poor-will description. It is very pretty and you may use it if you want to.

I haven't tried an air purifier for hay fever but may come to it. Have been holding off on the theory that I seldom stay in one room for than a few minutes at a time, even at night, and I'd have to buy about a dozen machines. My fever has subsided for 1960. It was bad in June though. I hope your back is mending.

Yrs.,
Whitey

November 21, 1960

Dear Whitey:

I see it is three months and three weeks since I should have thanked you for your definitive letter about sore backs and therapy for them, complete with addresses. How I hurt my back was falling 56 feet down the shaft of a tunnel about 1921. I hit the sides of the shaft several times on the descent and so got out of it with nothing worse than three cracked vertebrae, or "transverse process" I believe they're called in the back trade. There was some muscle and disc damage, which nails me when I do the wrong things—as described in yours of Aug. 2. When I'm nailed it's wicked, and I think of trusses. Then I get well and think I'm an athlete. I got well right after your letter came, and late in September took a long canoe trip down the Allagash River to Fort Kent with Justice Douglas and our wives. We had a hell of a fine time. 145 miles with pole, paddle. and the U.S. Supreme Court is one way to cure a back.

And now I am writing for another address—or information. It's with regard to chickens, We have just drawn plans for and are beginning work on a henhouse, for about two dozen birds. We have always remembered how delicious were the birds you and Katharine fed us at North Brooklin, and we understood that part of their flavor might have been due to feeding the fowl with non-medicated, non antibiotic grain. Once in a while in the big markets you buy a chicken that tastes like arnica, a thing we want to avoid. But we hear that nowadays most feed is full of medicines of various kinds. Do you know if you can buy the pure stuff, and if so, where? Or maybe you raised your own? Anyway, Mary's ambition is to produce a chicken that will taste as good as the Whites', and any dope you can hand out to advance this cause will be appreciated. We know your kitchen staff had plenty to do with the goodness of the chicken, but Mary thinks the feed did, too.

Did you ever see a better or longer fall season in Maine? Or anywhere, for that matter? We are still eating lettuce out of our garden. What's the news from North Brooklin?

Yours,
Smitty
Damariscotta, Maine

Wednesday
23 Nov. 1960

Dear Smitty:

I'm delighted that your back has returned in strength and that you were able to subdue the Allagash.

You have come to the right man for information about chickens, but I don't know whether to send you my Instruction Sheet A, or my B, or my C. Are you planning simply a meat operation—which can be accomplished in a few short, busy weeks and then a deep freeze? Or are you thinking of a full-scale operation, with a pen of laying hens? I bristle with all kinds of helpful information for an incipient poultryman, I've been raising birds ever since I was a kid. I like it—which is a big help. My methods are old fashioned (see upcoming *New Yorker*, December 3 issue). I start with 75 day-old chicks in April and always have a flock of about 20 layers in my henpen in the barn. This is a full-scale though small-scale, operation—it means a brooder house, a brooder stove, a range shelter, a range fence, a hen pen, and an egg-grading department down cellar. In the old happy days, my surplus eggs (about 8 dozen per week) could just be tossed into a handy carton and presented to the store for credit. Not anymore. Eggs turned in to a store, or sold to a retail customer, have to be candled and graded and packaged.

I have been fighting the matter of medicated feed for a long while. No bird of mine eats a lot of drugs, antibiotics, or other trash. I get a mash from Wirthmore called "Grow and Egg," and it is non-medicated. I also feed a small amount of scratch grain.

But I can't write about chickens today—the subject is too vast and interesting. One way you can do, if you want to have a laying flock but don't want to go to the trouble of brooding young chicks, is to buy "started" birds. I get my chicks from Parmenter, Inc., Franklin, Mass., and they have always done well by me. I always buy cross-bred birds. I have had the Sex-link Blacks, the Buff Cross, the Silver White Cross, and right now my pen of layers are a cross called Massachusetts Whites. All these crosses are brown-egg birds.

I'll write you more about chickens in a few days. Meantime, if you or Mary will drop me a card telling me whether your program calls for meat *and* eggs, or just meat, I'll be able to be of more help. K and I leave for New York by car day after tomorrow (Friday), so drop your card to the *New Yorker*.

Yrs.,
Whitey

P.S. Of the 75 chicks that I start, half (approx.) are male, half female. After about eight weeks, I select 22 pullets for my replacement flock and put them out on grass. This leaves 53 birds still in my brooder house. Of these, I give 18 to the fellow who works for me. This leaves 35. These are our broilers, fryers, and roasters. We start killing and freezing them as soon as they are broiler size, saving always enough for our immediate table demands. During the summer, we use fowl from the hen pen for jellied chicken (our finest dish) and thus start whittling down the old flock.

Nov. 24, 1960

Dear Whitey:

Your letter of yesterday is something to be thankful for. It's right from the grain bin. We are glad to know, first, about Wirthmore's feed; and second, to learn about the White Poultry System. Our bulldozer man, whose name is Oliver Wendell Holmes, has dumped and leveled eleven loads of gravel over our hen area. And we are about to lay the sills on a 12' × 12' henhouse, with adequate space off one end and one side for considerably larger yards, under fence.

What we have in mind is to inhabit the house with about thirty laying pullets. We had favored White Rocks, since they did so well by us, for eating and eggs, throughout our short "Outermost House" operation at the cabin. But I think now we'll write your man Parmenter in Franklin, Mass., for the Massachusetts Whites when the time comes. We like white birds and brown eggs. We intend to sell surplus eggs to a few pedigreed friends. And we figured on raising enough broilers for our own use, with started birds, no brooder. We hadn't gone as far in our thinking as "jellied chicken," but we'll probably be hitting you for the recipe one of these days.

I knew you were an accomplished poultryman, but didn't realize you'd made it a life work. (How did you happen to take up writing as a sideline?) Your zeal is contagious. With you as consultant, I don't see how we can miss. Thanks for your counsel, and we eagerly await more of it. I'll get the Dec. 3rd *New Yorker* and go right into research.

Yrs ever,
Smitty

Wednesday

FLASH

Twelve by twelve is OK. You may proceed pending further instructions relative to lighting, ventilation (insulation vs. no insulation), roosts and dropping board, nests (dark vs. open), litter (deep vs. shallow), position of door, location of windows and slide, design of hopper and waterer, and broody coop. Program outlined is fuzzy (gradually nibbling away at a laying flock during periods of hunger) but am powerless to do anything about that. Delighted to hear that Holmes is at work with a bulldozer. There is no point in living in the country unless you raise the devil; when I was thinking of getting a cow years ago, I started by acquiring some sticks of dynamite. A bulldozer is the thing, to get ready for a hen.

In haste,
Whitey

Progress Report
Mark II Henhouse

Dec. 3, 1960

Dear Whitey:

Your flash on chickens was OK, but your work on TV in the magazine ran smack into National Alcoholics Information Week. (Stay young fair and debonair. Be Sociable. Have a Pepsi.) Anyway, we think you put the needle right into the heart of the TV business. A fine, thoughtful exploration. Many local characters are extolling it, including me.

The National Alcoholics Information Week people said if the stuff interfered with your work you were an alcoholic. What I say is, you can't work on a henhouse in 28 degree weather with the wind blowing if you're more than eighty feet from a bottle. Just knowing it's there on a sturdy shelf gives you hope, and courage to drive twenty-penny nails into your two-by-fours. When darkness falls, you have just enough strength left to make it to the jug.

Sills, double floor (tar paper between), framing, and boarding up of one wall are now complete. I enclose plan. We hope to get the roof on over the weekend. Height of house at peak is eight feet. There is a porch, 3 × 12, long the south side for sitting and observing the hens. (Height of house from floor to plate is 6 feet 3 inches.) Insulation on north side, where nests and roosts will be located. Clapboards over tar paper on the other three sides. Outside paint is to be red with white trim, unless you think it will offend the birds. Inside, just the bare, clean pine.

I wish you could get here for an on-the-spot consultation. Bring a recipe for chapped hands.

Gratefully yours,
Smitty
Damariscotta, Maine

Pearl Harbor Day
Dec. 7, 1960

Dear Smitty:

If I were standing over you with a claw bar in one hand and a drink in the other, I would probably insist on certain changes in your grand design. But at this distance and all unarmed I feel helpless, and also I don't want to be responsible for anything that happens in Damariscotta. The sensible thing for me to do at this critical juncture is to sketch the hen pen in my own barn—a cubicle that has proved itself over twenty years in all weather—and let you glimpse perfection and then use your own judgment. Offhand I would say that your hen shebang is all right except you've got too god damn many doors and windows. You are all doors and windows, just the way I am all thumbs. And I would put my roosts on the North wall, and put my nests on the East wall—eliminating that full-size door and one window on the East. Why do you want a full door from the house to the yard? A pophole is all you need, and you can enter the yard through its own wire door outside if you want to. I am a dark nest man from away back. No breakage, cleaner, better conditions. And they are not hard to build—mostly out of half-inch stuff.

The vital wall in any hen house is the South wall. Mine, as you see, has a big opening—about 3' × 5' fitted with a slide—and two fixed windows. The big opening stays open night and day, winter, summer, spring, and fall except in a driving storm from the SE, when I close it to keep out rain or snow. In other words, the inside of my henpen is the same temperature as the outside world, give or take a couple of degrees. This prevents (or I think prevents) condensation and dampness. I also cut a round hole in the roof, near the highest point, and fitted a galvanized iron ventilator with its little hat. There are a million theories about henhouse ventilation, but the White theory, known as White's Law, is that you should never close the place up. To me a henhouse stands or falls on whether it can stay dry and cheerful during the cold, dark winter months. (Anybody can keep hens dainty in summer.)

I am a deep-litter man. My hen pen gets serviced only once a year, and when it gets serviced it gets serviced good. I prefer dropping boards to manure pits. I had manure pits in my big henhouse years ago, when I was keeping hens in quantity, and I never cared for those pits. In my hen pen I simply built a plain table about the height of an ordinary desk, and this serves as the dropping boards. Over it are the roosts. Welded wire, 1" × 4", makes a fine covering for the roost frame, and then on top of that you set the poles or two-by-fours that the birds sit on. My roost frame is hinged to the North wall in such a way that I can wing it up in the air while I scrape the droppings into a basket. I do this once a week and it works fine. (Hen manure, incidentally, is great stuff if properly fortified and properly diluted, but it is a very strong medicine.)

I house my pullets around October 1, and they go in a clean whitewashed pen, with about six to eight inches of litter on the floor. This litter never gets changed for one year. It gets pushed around once in a while—stirred up—but you don't remove it. If the litter stays dry, the hens stay healthy and the eggs are 99 percent clean shelled—immaculate. If the litter gets soggy and nasty, anything can happen. Dirty eggs are caused by a hen's feet being dirty. Dry feet are clean feet.

The best litter is a mixture of "Servall" (sugar cane husks) and wood shavings. *Don't use sawdust.* You can buy Servall from your grain man by the bale (you'll need two bales). And if he says he hasn't got it, beat him over the head with threats: No Servall for Smitty, Smitty no buy grain. Get a load of dry shavings from your mill and mix the two together on the floor of the house. It's a lovely mixture. Servall is extremely absorptive, and shavings are nice and noisy and bright. I guess I better add right here that it is not safe to start a bunch of hens on deep litter in the dead of winter, because the stuff might suddenly get very wet, not having been properly kneaded and worked up by the birds.

A hen will lay in anything—a chamber pot, an orange crate, a derby hat. But for best results, build a double deck of dark nests along one wall. A dark nest is simply a nest that the hen enters from the rear instead of from the front. Eggs are collected through hinged doors in the front. In order for the hens to enter from the rear, the nests of course have to be set out from the wall about nine inches, and a walkway provided for them, which is just a board laid on the brackets that hold the whole structure. I like double nests rather than single, i.e., each nest is about 12" × 22". I use wood shavings for nesting material. The roof of the nest bank must slope sharply, so the birds don't use it for a parade ground. And the board that forms the back of the nests must be only about five inches wide, so the hen can step into the nest without chinning herself.

Hell, I've got to stop thinking about chickens and go to work. Good luck, farmer.

Yrs.,
Whitey

P.S. Would the Allagash be a good subject for a feature movie, on the Save-the-Wilderness theme? Friend of mine, who made the lobster film for TV, is thinking about the Allagash. If we could get him in one canoe and Justice in another, it might be fun to watch from the bank.

I'll be home on Friday.

Examination Paper No. 3
The White Correspondence Course
Henhouse Division

Dec. 11, 1960

Dear Whitey:

Yesterday I'm sixty. I moved into your age group. I take my place there confidently. My henhouse bears the mark of White, the big door on the east wall having been transformed into a hop-hole, which I assume is a relatively small aperture through which the hens hop to their outdoor yard and back in again. I have also been won over to having roosts and nests on separate walls, and your drawing of the dark nest construction is irresistible. I shall enjoy constructing them, as well at the White dropping board.

When I started building, I foresaw that I would be banging up fingers and thumbs with the hammer, so I went into Perley Waltz's drugstore where the following dialog took place.

Smitty: "Gimme enough Bandaids to build a henhouse."

Perley: "How big is the henhouse?'

Smitty: "Twelve by twelve."

Perley: "Better take three boxes."

I am now into my last box. All boarded up, roof on and papered with ninety-pound, grainy surfaced paper, posts all set for the yard. Clapboarding is the next job. But I am also thinking of copying your south wall opening. I may settle for a Dutch door deal. And I may board up the door on the West wall. I am flexible, rolling with the punches.

I forgot to tell you that originally we planned a multiple-use house—one that could turn into a shelter for grandchildren, or a remount station for the summer traveler, the uninvited type. But we now see by reason of your counsel that a henhouse is a henhouse, and nothing else. We are proceeding with this as policy, and to hell—as I have said repeatedly—with the summer traveler.

There's one thing you ought to know: my henhouse is the only one in the world that has been photographed by a former U.S. ambassador to Egypt and Israel. The Ambassador has taken pictures of our structures in two stages, and when the prints come I'll send you copies as evidence that I'm not just fooling around with a dream. I have a second distinction: I am the only man anywhere in these parts with E. B. White as a henhouse consultant. If my hens catch the spirit of all this, I'll be eating eggs by the first of February, 1961.

Yrs. with optimism and gratitude,
Smitty
Damariscotta, Maine

P.S. I should think the Allagash would be a honey for the Save-The-Wilderness theme. And Justice Bill is for saving it. However, I have a hunch he may have other wildernesses to suggest. Why don't you have your TV film friend write to him? Just address him at the U.S. Supreme Court, Wash., D.C. He's very amenable to this sort of thing. Smitty

Dec. 14, 1960
Maine

I imagine most of the paper blew off your henhouse day before yesterday. Sorry about this, but these setbacks are inevitable in this business. Don't lose your nerve. Your February 1 date for first egg sounds too early and as though you were working under pressure. I would down-date entire program and step up drinking, allowing more time at end of day. Forty-five years in poultry has convinced me that patience is the number one virtue. Lesson 4 follows as soon as I get plowed out.

On a typed note card

Instructions for Installing
White's Little Daisy Non-Self-Filling Shell & Grit Feeder

1. Select a suitable location on wall of henhouse.
2. Cause two nails to be driven into the wall, cunningly, at the height of 16½ inches from the floor, and so spaced that the head of each nail will penetrate and support its own staple on the Little Daisy.
3. Fill right-hand compartment with oyster shell, left-hand compartment with grit pounded from Maine granite. NEVER reverse this order, as the Feeder will not work, and the hens will become alarmed, ill-natured, and unproductive.

December 26, 1960

Dear Whitey:

Lesson Four, in the form of White Little Daisy Non-Self-Filling Shell & Grit Feeder, arrived in fine shape to put our Christmas on a high plane. The Little Daisy occupied a position on our living-room table between a bottle of rum labelled "Old Doctor Smith's Golden Medical Discovery" and a box of golf balls. The Little Daisy attracted more attention than even the rum, many visitors figuring it was some new kind of crèche, the double-ceremony type. Jake Day, the artist, has promised me a sack of oyster shells and some Maine granite grit. I am damn near in business, or at least running nicely in the stretch.

The Ambassador was down to photograph the current building stage, and I believe he used up his film roll, so you should be having the evidence before too long.

I tried stepping up drinking yesterday, acting on your postcard instructions, but I should have stuck to gin and coke, a known benefactor, instead of drinking eggnogs. The nogs poured like pancake batter—the only drink within memory that called for toothpicks afterward. The result of the stepped-up drinking is not your fault. Besides, I will be all right after another hour, when I will be out working on the Whitehouse.

We were pleased, in fact delighted, by the card from you, Katharine & hens. This sort of thing spurs me on.

Thanks for the Little Daisy. Installation, according to your instruction sheet, will soon take place. Happy New Year to your and yours.

Yrs., gratefully
Smitty

North Brooklin
9 Jan. 1961

Dear Smitty:

I imagine you are about halfway through building dark nests and
are sore as hell at me for ever suggesting them. Last night I lay
awake worrying about you and dark nests and trying to figure out
a way to explain their construction, but I couldn't think of anything except to tell you to play it by ear—feel your way through
this crisis. I got so wakeful I got out of bed at three thirty, visited
the refrigerator and the liquor closet, knocked myself out with
whiskey and milk, and was up again at six preparing to drive to
Bangor for a 9:45 appointment with an eye doctor. My wife also
had an appointment, and she took her newly drafted last will
and testament along, so that we could stop in Ellsworth at my
bank to sign the document in front of witnesses.

We lunched at the Penobscot Exchange after the eye appoint-
ments, and during lunch I glanced down and discovered that the
zipper on my fly had let go. I tried making repairs by holding a
paper napkin over it with one hand and fiddling with the other,
but got nowhere except that I think I aroused the interest of a
couple of the waitresses, one of whom seemed ready to report me
on a morals charge. After lunch, I walked stiff-leggedly from the
room and went downstairs to the Men's, where I continued to try
easing the little slide back onto its track. But it was hopeless—
this zipper had gone off its trolley with every intention of staying
off. So we continued to Ellsworth, where Katharine entered the
bank carrying her Will and I stayed in the car, hiding, like the
decent fellow I am. Katharine was back in a flash to report that
the officers of my bank had cold-shouldered her, had questioned
her identity, had asked her why I hadn't accompanied her, and

had refused to produce witnesses unless *she* could produce *me*. (I should explain that K doesn't bank at this institution but at some fly-by-night outfit in New York called by the implausible name of Morgan Guaranty Trust Company.) Anyway, I said I would be goddamned if I'd escort her into my bank with an open fly, and she said she would be goddamned if she'd go home without signing the will—which I suspect is cutting me off without a penny or she wouldn't be so hot to get it on record. We kicked this back and forth for a while, and finally I let her have her way. I walked into the bank and past the teller's cages as though I had Charley Horses in both legs, and when we reached the directors' room, where all tribal rituals are held in this bank, Mr. Austin produced two females and Katharine was so flustered by the whole business she started to write "ninth" where she should have written "January" and had to scrawl the January all over the word ninth, and I just stood there wondering how much of me was visible, and the others staring at me and wondering why I had been so recalcitrant about attending the rites. I doubt that the will would stand up in court, the way Katharine was lousing it up with the pen. But I figure that what a bank doesn't know won't hurt it, or a witness either. And now back to dark nests.

Mine are set 7 inches from the wall, which is enough. And the bottom tier is 20 inches off of the floor, which is enough. I think the sketch I sent you showed the nests supported by a diagonal brace to the wall, but I believe the simplest construction is to set two posts, from floor to rafters, and build from them. A two-by-two makes a nice-sized post. I think that the fundamental problem that confronts a man who is about to build dark nests is whether to build the nests first and then the frame, or build the frame first and then fit the nests to the frame. A man could spend the better part of a winter tossing that around, without ever lifting a hammer. My nests are 13 inches wide. The headroom is 14 inches. All you really have to do is build two long boxes, or coffins, set a couple of partitions in at appropriate places, omit the top board on the backside so the hen can stop into the nest, and hinge the top board on the front side to the owner can collect the eggs!

And I think it's time now you began to worry about slipped tendons, vent gleet, bacillary white diarrhea, prolapse of the oviduct, omphalitis (navel ill), necrosis of the beak, mycosis of the digestive tract (thrush), leukosis, limber neck, and the mite—red, scaly-leg, and feather.

Let me know how things are going.

Yrs.,
Whitey

January 11, 1961

Dear Whitey:

Don't worry about my henhouse. I just want you to get it off your mind for a while, because that zipper is enough trouble for any man at one time, and then you have Katharine's will on top of that; and still on top of that is the second waitress. You say "I think I aroused the interest of a couple of waitresses, one of whom seemed ready to report me on a morals charge." It's the other one that fills me with apprehension. What was the interest aroused in her? It all fits in with the dark nest theme. I could build a dark nest with mahogany gunwales—just give me the word on how far you want it from the wall, dimensions of escape hatch and other essentials.

Almost the most apropos thing I ever heard in the above connection is the name of the photographer who made the prints from the Ambassador's pictures of the stages of development of the Whitey-Smitty henhouse. I hope to get the prints tomorrow on my town trip to enclose with this letter. I shall also enclose evidence that the print-maker's name is Ivan Fly. Everything hooks up but the zipper. It makes a hell of a neat world.

I am all clear, Whitey, on the dark nest construction. You have given me headroom, floor or laying space dimension, and the catwalk, or birdwalk, size, and the hinge arrangements. As for how to frame it, mount it in the house, and like that, it's a problem I go to sleep with—a productive substitute for counting sheep. I wake up in the morning and know just what to do, although sometimes I mess it up and am driving nails through the air.

Today I have completed the hophole, which lures the group from house to open yard. It's a hooded thing, hooded to keep out wetness in driving rains, and lovely to behold. I'm putting in a few tank traps so the birds won't think it's a nesting place. (The hood is actually only 14 inches long—just a covered bridge to sunshine.)

At this moment, I am about ready to start the dark nest construction. I can do this in a full, strong day if I don't get bothered by the Detroit nemesis. Then the roosts and the dropping board. I have your plans on these and they are well in mind.

Waterers and feeders are next on the agenda. We have a nice Wirthmore man in Wiscasset. But if you have advice on this subject for a thirty-bird man, give me the business in the Poultry Correspondence Course—it would be about Lesson Five, now, I think.

In two weeks, which discounts a wedding of a prized niece over in New Hampshire, we shall be ready for the Massachusetts Whites from the Parmenter people in Franklin, Mass. Do they ship? And how? We are leaping in to the kill, Whitey! I may make that February first date yet. I am calloused, lean, haughty, and serene. Guys are offering me fifty bucks a week for rent for my henhouse in summer-hazard season. No sale. This joint is for Massachusetts Whites. We wish to hell the North Brooklin White would come and see what they've had a finger in—nay, a whole arm.

As for my diseases, I am ready to face them. I have a touch, myself, of bacillary white diarrhea due to eating creamed onions, which I love; and my necrosis of the beak is due either to frostbite from working in zero weather on the henhouse, or to gin and Coke. So far, no prolapse of the oviduct or mycosis of the digestive tract.

Can't you get that zipper fixed and come down and see the house? Christ, Whitey, come anyway. Mary and I could witness the latest will and testament, and you would have access to the milk and liquor cupboard at three in the morning, or just simple breath in the afternoon if you'd prefer. This mail-order henhouse needs your eye and the curled lip of the pro as he scans the creation of the eager amateur.

As an added attraction, we have some imported beef equal to your jellied chicken, or even the ones you served for lunch so long ago just inside the terrace. How are things on the campus of your correspondence school? Come on down and tell.

Yours,
Smitty
Damariscotta, Maine

P.S. We'll be away for that wedding over the coming weekend; but after that, when the light gets long in the afternoons, I hope we can somehow arrange a viewing. I mean, inspection. Smitty

Sunday, Jan. 15, 1961

Dear Smitty:

Thanks for the photographs, which I find highly diverting. Your henhouse is less beautiful than Chartres but almost as intricate. I have never seen such a window-and-door-happy couple as you and your wife. I can discover hardly an inch of available wall space, and I don't know where your hens are going to hang their pictures. But I think everybody is going to be very happy with this fine structure and I congratulate you.

Am enclosing some snapshots of a proper henpen, with Massachusetts Whites at rest and at play. Two of the snaps show the south facade, with opening and slide (made of sheeting). Another snap shows the terrace in the winter. Another my bull calf. Every henpen should have a white-faced calf knocking about, to give it tone, and I'm sure yours soon will.

Before I forget it, I want to tell you that Massachusetts Whites are not an all-white bird. Some are completely white, others show a few reddish feathers, mostly on wings and breast. I think they're rather pretty, but if you're looking for all-white plumage, they are not your dish.

I'd love to accept your kind invitation to visit Damariscotta and pull you out of this mess, but I am not free to leave home. Right now we are marking time and are also about to receive two young grandchildren for a short visit, while our son and his wife go to New York.

If you've recovered from the wedding and are still game to try dark nests, you will find enclosed an operational set of plans, treacherous as the devil but well-intentioned and drawn with agonizing difficulty by a man who can't do mechanical drawings but likes to Think Things Through. As you become more and more engrossed in this 3-step method that I have worked out for you, I believe you will begin to appreciate its simplicity, its inner beauty, and its exquisite miscalculations. Good luck, and God go with you.

You will be so exhausted, after completing the house and the nests, you won't have the strength to build the White Non-Fouling No-Waste Feeder and the White Waterer, based on the two-pail winter-proof system, so I shall try to get to work on these in my workshop. It will take my mind off my troubles, and if you don't like them, they will make excellent kindling. I don't know how I'll get them to you, but I will.

Whitey

White's 3-Step Method

Operation #1—Starting the Frame.
1. Pick a suitable location, to give you about 6' length, 24" depth.
2. Set two small posts, floor to roof, 24" from wall, extreme measure.
3. Abandon framing and go to.

Operation #2—Building the Nesting Unit.
1. Measure the distance between posts, inside measure. If the distance is, say, 70 inches, then let 70 inches (lean) be the length of your nesting unit. When you get through building this unit, it should *just* slide into place between the posts and rest on the crosspiece, see sheet #1.
2. Build unit. See sheet #2 . Cleat two boards together to make the ends, cleats being on *inside*, Nail sides to ends, then nail bottom to ends, flush with sides. The middle cleat should

be in the right place to support the bottom of the top deck of nests. Set two partitions into each deck, dividing each deck into three nests. These partitions had better be ¾" boards, for good nailing. Nail everything together in good shape (I like galvanized clapboard nails when I am using half-inch stuff). Remember not to nail home the boards that will be hinged, for access of owner.

3. Study everything to discover where Whitey has made his first ghastly error in calculations. Correct this error. It may mean burning down the building.

4. Pour rum over ice and drink it.

Operation #3—Setting the Unit.

1. Slide unit between posts, boost it up till it is about 20" off the floor, and hold it there by shoveling something under it temporarily. See if the height is OK as to extension of roof-line, that is, do you have enough height of wall. If everything looks all right, proceed with framing.

2. Nail the two lower crosspieces from wall to post, nailing them to the INSIDE of the posts. These crosspieces will support the nesting unit and will also support the walkway. See sheet #1.

3. Using nesting unit as a guide, fit the diagonal top crosspieces, wall to post, nailing them to the OUTSIDE of the posts. These will be your little rafters for finishing the roof.

4. Set middle crosspieces, nailing them to OUTSIDE of posts. These will support the upper walkway.

5. Fit the walkways. The lower one had better be a little longer than the upper one. Each should extend out a few inches beyond the unit. Use your judgment here. This will be the "Smith" touch to the structure.

6. There is no need to nail the nesting unit to the frame, but I would fasten it to the posts with 4 screws, two in each post to steady it. Then if you ever want to remove it, you can just remove the screws and slide the unit out.

January 26, 1961

Dear Whitey:

Despite your cruel thrust about my henhouse being less beautiful than Chartres but almost as intricate, I want you to share in the knowledge that the dark nests are a reality—a bit of architecture installed. You can touch it, smell the clean pine, see the heads of cleanly driven nails, follow in your mind's eye the progress of the laying birds on walkways one and two. White's Laws were violated only by way of amendments here and there to meet the Smith decor—Smith Variations, they are called. But the vital, White measurements rule all, and with a little encouragement I could lay an egg myself in Tier Two, Nest Three. Your plans were a great help, as well as a responsibility which has been discharged with faith in the architect.

We went down to Wiscasset yesterday to the Wirthmore people. They have Servall, non-medicinal grain, baled shavings, and all the stuff you prescribe. They deliver, and we have established credit. They must have seen the light in our eyes.

We have also, today, sent off a letter to Parmenter, Inc., of Franklin, Mass., stating that you recommended them as a source of birds of character and breeding. We enclosed a self-addressed and stamped envelope to facilitate their early reply as to when they can ship. Meanwhile, I have only to construct roosts and dropping board (I have your notes on these). If all goes well, I'll miss the first-egg deadline by about a week—a moral victory, considering the weather in which your client has been working. There are cracks in my fingers as deep as the Grand Canyon.

You should know the reason why houses I build run to doors and windows. I need places through which to see, breathe, and flee. I assume my animals are like-minded. Many people call me an escapist—that word!—little realizing that it is sound to get away from something you hate to something you love, or hate less. You remove your palm from a hot stove. It's escape. You go from Detroit or New York to wilderness Maine. Escape. They say in effect that to be where you do not like to be is noble, to be where you like to be, ignoble and suspect. A few of the people who have called me an escapist are in institutions. Me, I am in and out of a damn fine henhouse, and I can get in and out from three directions

The pictures of your Massachusetts Whites and their home have had scrutiny. That young bull calf looks fine, too. So does the woodpile.

I'll try to get dark nest pictures to you soon; and you should see the installation of White's Little Daisy Non-Self-Filling Shell & Grit Feeder. I haven't actually got her on the wall yet, but the time is practically here.

Things are fine here under the long arm of Whitey.

Yours,
Smitty

Saturday, January 28, 1961

Dear Smitty:

Just got your letter and am glad things are going well.

If you haven't sent your order in, for ready-to-lay birds (and I guess you have), you should consider the alternative of buying "started" birds, about six or seven weeks old. I know you are hot to pick up an egg out of those beautiful nests, but there is much to be said for buying younger chickens. If you want broilers and fryers in your freezer, that is the way to get them. A "ready-to-lay" pullet has gone by the broiler-fryer stage and is in the roaster stage, and will soon be an old fowl. You can buy, say, 50 started chicks, seven weeks old, feed them for a couple of weeks, and then kill a dozen or more for broilers. A little later, harvest the roasting birds, put them in the freezer, and you would still be left with a nice laying flock—except they wouldn't be laying for a while. I imagine I am too late with this bit of advice, and perhaps it is unwelcome anyway. Every man should do what he damn pleases when it comes to hens, and not listen to cranks.

I want to warn you about litter at this season of the year, and in an untried henhouse. If it were me, I'd lay down only a very thin coat of litter on the floor, and every day I would add three or four bushels of the stuff. Then if you find you have a damp-litter problem, you will not have lost all your good material. For some reason or other, litter has to be well busted up before it really works, and the birds are the ones to bust it up. Feed a quart and a half of scratch grain at the edge of dark, when it's still light enough for the birds to pick it up. If you *should* decide to buy young chickens, instead of laying birds, there is just one thing you've got to watch: the first couple of nights, you and your wife will have to be on hand at bedtime in the henhouse, to tuck the children in for the night. They might just go off in a corner, crowd themselves like a subway mob, and suffocate. All you have to do is ladle them up onto the roosts and stand by until they accept the location. It's not hard if the house is fairly dark.

I've built you a Cornell waterer that you can use if you like it, and I'm going to build you a feeder someday, if I ever get in the clear again. We leave on Wednesday for New York, and K goes into the hospital Feb 4, to take tests. We are booked to go to Sarasota, but have no idea whether or not we will be able to go.

Yrs.,
Whitey

P.S. Perhaps you should ask a real honest-to-God poultryman about litter. I've never had a henhouse-warming at this time of year, and so cannot talk from experience.

February 14, 1961

Dear Whitey:

I don't know where you are, or if Katharine is okay—but I hope you are both in Sarasota, enjoying the sun. And I hope this letter overtakes you. It's a Valentine loaded with important news.

Yesterday, at 2:00 P.M.—a fine, sunny afternoon—a man drove up to our henhouse in a smart ranch wagon containing thirty, seventeen-week-old Massachusetts Whites. He was, of course, from Parmenter's and his name—no kidding—is Peckham. So what we did was a straddle from young birds (started birds?) to adolescents. The group should lay its first egg April first, which is what you figured was about right all along.

Mr. Peckham was very happy about the birds' new home, which of course pleased us. We put down about four inches of Servall and wood chips in equal parts. The Little Daisy is installed at your prescribed altitude of 16½ inches, and the shell is on the right, the grit on the left, as per your Christmas instruction sheet. And a letter from Ray Parmenter says, "Remember me to Mr. White—an old friend."

The group crowded into a corner of the henhouse last night, and we tenderly unsnarled them, put them on the roosts, and they put in a good night, only to wake up this morning and find a southeast snowstorm whistling at their eaves. But they are dry, reasonably warm, tactfully ventilated, and—at this writing—a solid joy. They are very pretty, we think, and feminine, running in color from almost pure white to an attractive strawberry roan.

Mr. Peckham praised the dark nests, the roosts, which swing up and hook to the ceiling by a chain (White's New Departure for easy dropping-board scraping), and the Little Daisy. He okayed the litter and ventilation and returned—reluctantly, we thought—to Franklin.

The Ambassador is coming down this afternoon, via snowplow as it now looks, for inspection and gin. He is a man who carefully wipes his feet before stepping into a henhouse and also after stepping out of one.

I will try to have him, or someone, get some pictures of the interior and the birds, as trophies. It is wonderful to have this climax in a project. Next climax, the first egg. Mary is betting on April Fool's day. The White Correspondence Course, Poultry Division, has already paid off in enjoyment.

I'm sending this to North Brooklin, and it will probably get quite a ride before it reaches you; but we hope it finds you both well. Pick an orange for me, okay, Whitey?

Yours,
Smitty

Sarasota

Mar. 3, 1961

Dear Smitty:

Thanks for the letter, which I hope to answer soon. Katharine not well.

Whitey

On a hand-written postcard of an aerial view of St. Armands.

Picked an orange today.

Regards
Whitey

On a hand-written postcard of oranges and blossoms in Sarasota.

March 18, 1961
Fiddlers Bayou
Sarasota, Florida
Saturday

Dear Smitty:

I hope your girls are well. They will get very flighty and nervous just before coming into lay, and will go straight up into the air if you make a sudden motion, like looking at your wristwatch to see whether it is lunchtime. This flightiness lasts several weeks, usually. Incidentally, I'm not starting chicks this spring. Have ordered started birds from Ray Parmenter, scheduled to arrive at my place May 1.

My girl is not well at all. She will have to go into the hospital again in April for more tests. She is apprehensive about the future, but not dispirited. Finds it very hard to do any sustained mental work, and this makes her ripping mad. Our weather has been gorgeous, and I've managed to get in a swim every day. But I spend a lot of time as a practical (or impractical) nurse.

Yrs.,
Whitey

March 21, 1961

Dear Whitey:

From yours of Saturday, it appears that at least the medicine men know what ails Katharine and have some idea of how to make her well. For what it may be worth, please tell Katharine that "sustained mental work" is for me a memory, and not an especially happy one at that. I hold that the human brain is the most inefficient machine ever devised, and that the labor of writing is man's more disorganized endeavor. The wastebaskets I have filled with paper covered by mistakes, if left standing in the original spruce, would forest a wilderness. Maybe this isn't going to cheer Katharine at all. As her nurse, you shall judge.

Just as you said. The girls are beginning to act nervous. We have had two casualties, leukosis victims, about four weeks apart. The remaining twenty-eight are a joy—fine, patrician birds. Now and then a couple of them jump up to inspect the dark nests, and it is pleasant to note their appreciation of my craftsmanship. We are giving them a little scratch every evening before bedtime. The litter is dry and clean. Only about ten days to first egg day.

A lot of snow here—close to ten inches, and still cold and drafty outdoors. I like to have you in Maine, where you belong, but you better stick around to Sarasota for a while longer. Besides, I think there are some good doctors in the Medical Arts Center there. We had a little place just south of Venice, but the people and the country seemed awful flat to us and we cleared out.

Out of the blue the other day a charming and intelligent young couple showed up with an apology for intruding and high praise for my literary efforts, which they had read. Mr. and Mrs. Richard Aldridge, their name is—and he is a poet, and a damn good one, published by Indiana University Press, which I have heard is quality. I had settled down happily listening to compliments and basking in self-esteem when young Aldridge mentioned E. B. White. At that point Smitty got lost, and all they talked about was you, and everything they said was good. They are damn discriminating people, too, and we wound up a splendid afternoon with a henhouse inspection during which several birds pointed out with their beaks the White Little Daisy Non-Self-Refilling Grit & Shell Feeder.

Best to you and K.

Yours,
Smitty

March 21, 1961

Dear Whitey:

Follow-up: When I went up to town this morning to mail a letter to you and to get my incoming mail, I dialed my P.O. box open, reached in and found a tiny live chick peeping from the semi-confinement of the folds of the *Saturday Evening Post*. This was a "presentation" from the Damariscotta Post Office crew, signalizing my entry into the poultry world. Shows you how much interest is being created around here. The chick was tenderly replaced in someone's shipment from Sears Roebuck. It had been borrowed for the moment of my un-hinging Box 372. You don't get this kind of Post Office service in Detroit, perhaps not even Sarasota.

Yours ever,
Smitty

P.S. Just now, at scratch feeding time, a couple of the girls were squatting in the characteristic pose of expecting a rooster. This augurs well for the first egg, I should think. Smitty

And there's another thing you ought to know: The wind has stilled down, the shadows lying out long on the snow, and it's fun walking out around on the place and having the feeling of caring for it and its creatures. That ought to make you damn good and homesick.

April 17, 1961

Dear Smitty:

I've been a bad correspondent—have been too busy doubling as a practical nurse. (My wife drops things and I pick them up.) But the news this morning is encouraging. A second neurological look at her seems to indicate that there is no tumor, and that the irritation to the nerves is of a less ominous sort. You can fire your rifle 21 times in the air for me; mine is out of reach.

Glad to hear your birds are shelling out. The deluxe non-fouling non-frost-proof waterer that I built for you last fall from almost-clear pine still awaits delivery. And my offer still holds good to build you a Sensible Feeder. But first I have to pry Katharine out of Harkness, wash her long green hair (one of the tests turns your hair green), drive her to Maine in our car, which today is somewhere on its way north from Sarasota probably driven by a man who likes to bump into little girls going 70, answer my mail, disinfect my bull calf's recent surgery, build several 16-inch picket fences to keep Augie out of the flower borders, and devise a way to recoup the fortune we lost this winter. *Then* I will build you a Sensible Feeder and you can substitute it for the thing I presume you now have in there, from which the Wirthmore mash sifts steadily out onto the floor under the ceaseless billing of the birds.

I also have to take a drink. K hasn't had a drink since January 3, and I have to do the work of two.

Yours,
Andy

April 23, 1961

Dear Andy:

The news about Katharine lifted an anvil off us, and what it must do for you and for her after that long anxiety calls for a song. High in the Ill Wind Dept. is your obligation to do the drinking for two. I hope you are discharging it manfully and without protest.

I can hardly wait to see how you built (from almost-clear pine) a deluxe non-fouling non-frost-proof waterer. Is the pine waterproof as well as knot-free? And the Sensible Feeder is something else to look forward to. You are a benefactor—more than you know.

In the May *Field & Stream* there's the story of our Allagash trip with Justice Douglas—or what the editors left of it after (probably) making room for a few columns of black and white ads. However, you will like the pictures, which are nuts.

Before I get on Massachusetts Whites, I want to report ownership of a new Falcon Ranch Wagon. You have never heard me rave about a car, unless against one, till now. I haven't really had any fun driving a car, before this Falcon, since I stole my father-in-law's Marmon around 1922. If I ever get to see you, and I hope I do, I'll let you drive it.

But the real rave is for the birds. They are clean, friendly, and sing a song of tranquility as we move about them. When you open the dark roost hatch and fish around underneath one of the birds for eggs, she turns around and looks at you as if glad to trade an egg for your attentions. It is wonderfully satisfying.

For a long time not a bird visited A-Deck—the top tier of nests. So we extended the launching pad, or walkway, on B-Deck for a better take-off angle, and now both decks are loaded every day. There are twenty-eight birds (we lost two—lukosis), and twice we have had twenty-*nine* eggs. But this included a couple of soft-shellers, kind of like turtle eggs.

We are selling to a few pedigreed friends, such as Julie and Edward Myers, and Jean Gannett Williams—only the highest types—and have over ten dollars in egg money already, or about three bottles of Gordon's Gin. This is a new, wonderful way of getting liquor out of corn, and I wish again to express my gratitude to you for your part in this caper. The fact that you can eat the eggs, and they, too, are wonderful, really wraps it up.

Would you ever consider writing something for the *Ford Times* under such working titles as: "What's in the Sea for Me," "How to Look at a Brook," or "How to See a Tree?" I am thinking of that tree on your place where the pileated drills and the raccoons gestate. If I promised never to ask you to write *Ford Times* stuff again, don't even do any considering. In any case, I wouldn't want it to interfere in any way with the production of the Sensible Feeder, as we are now using one of those metal things—a trough—and the girls whip their mash all over hell. The scratch-at-night deal keeps the litter light and fluffy, and we have one bird, a tall strawberry roan, who can snap the litter six or eight feet behind her with very low trajectory. The Flock consults the White Non-Self-Refilling Shell & Grit Feeder from time to time and they occasionally leave droppings in it which we carefully pluck out for our fertilizer pile, following our theory that one good turd deserves another.

Cheers for Katharine's recovery! Come home soon.

Yours ever,
Smitty
Damariscotta, Maine

22 May 1961

Smitty:

Your hen palace is constantly in my mind, but that's about all as of this date. Katharine is less well and spending most of her day abed, to forestall the headaches that come with the upright position. House is a disaster area because we are putting in a bathroom on the second floor to connect with guest room. Thanks for your letter of April 23—will reply as soon as the plaster dust clears away.

Whitey

On a blank, typed postcard.

June 17, 1961

Dear Whitey:

What with all the North Brooklin crises, you deserve some good news, and my news is terrible. The White Non-Self-Refillable Shell & Grit Feeder fell off the hen palace wall the other day and lay there on the litter. The staples, installed by you, were insecure. Who the hell isn't? Were you trying to make that point with those staples?

Over to Colby the 5th to hear Justice Douglas's fine commencement address, and had dinner and many highballs with Justice Bill that night. About the only flaw I can find in him is that he likes to tell dirty stories. This troubles me; but I can forgive it, because he loves the wilderness so passionately that he is categorically against human footprints. And he is in favor of good things, like Jack Daniels and human kindness. I think he qualifies as a great man.

Mary's lettuce plantation is a thing of beauty. There is quite a lot of serenity around the place, despite the fact that we are preparing for the August arrival of son Jim, daughter-in-law Avis, and grandsons Jeff, Stevie, and Mike. A man has promised to come and paint the house. I, personally, am painting the beautiful, Kentucky-type board fence that newly borders the road side of our domain. I've used two gallons of Dutch Boy Outside White already, and still have about a mile of fence to go. All I can think of is Tom Sawyer.

This is a mush year for hay, which reminds me that you will probably be going down to New York for the annual pollen count.

I hope things are fine with you, and that Katharine is improving, and the dust of the bathroom building and illness has cleared away.

Yours,
Smitty
Damariscotta, Maine

July 17, 1961

Dear Smitty:

Yours of June 17 at hand, but Katharine in hospital recuperating after an acute appendix operation. Jack Daniels and I have been keeping house alone for past week. My old hens chose this time of crisis to eat each other up. Will write some day.

Yrs.,
Whitey

On a hand-written blank postcard.

November 1, 1961

Dear Whitey:

Opening of deer season, God damn it.

Last word from you told of Katharine's acute appendectomy and you and Jack Daniels running the house alone. So your silence since that date (July 17) has been pretty ominous.

I had a lot of news I wanted to write you about—trips to Seattle, Washington, and D.C., the visit of my son, daughter-in-law, and three excellent grandsons, and how I fell off the porch roof of the henhouse, a free fall of six feet and four inches. Severe contusions and abrasions about the fanny and one elbow, still on exhibition only to intimate friends of either sex.

But none of this seemed very worthwhile, so I kept procrastinating; and then one of our *Ford Times* boys reported sighting you and James Thurber in the Algonquin a couple or more weeks ago; and my reporter said an Algonquin elevator operator told him Katharine was ill again; and then Thurber went to the hospital; so now I am wondering what is what, and how and where you are, and Katharine and Thurber, too.

One bright spot in all of this was when a friend of mine brought me the *N'Yer* with your elm and oriole story. I thought theme and execution both fine. Mary read *Charlotte's Web* this summer in between short-order cooking and gardening, and she loved it.

Another bright spot was a canoe trip Mary and I had on the Cains River in New Brunswick, a small wild river with a voice like sonnets. We got back the 7th of last month. One of the guides was a compulsive moose caller. Using a rolled piece of tar paper for a trumpet, we called moose from all over the Cains River wilderness right to our cabin doorstep—not one moose, but at least eight different ones, and at different times, of course. There isn't a happy bull moose left for miles around there. When they learned that the voice of love was of the stuff of tar paper, they just wandered off sadly, without even stepping on us. Maybe there ought to be an open season on moose callers.

Mary has a new Rolleiflex camera which she bought with her egg and lettuce money amassed this season. Our house, barn, henhouse, cats, visitors, and selves are by now well photographed in color, black and white, and sometimes gray. Mary has received acclaim from local experts. It's just a question of time before she gets into *Life*. I can then retire and spend the golden years investing her checks in Central Maine Power.

My literary life and labor has produced—harder and harder—a sound bit on homesickness, which, as applied to tourists originated in the heart of the American hobo, the first hitchhikers, of which I was one. My pitch is that the return trip, the trip home, is the journey with the real heart and true destination.

Then I contrived a book review, by command of the Gannett newspapers, of Justice Douglas's *East to Katahdin*. My review, although good, is so inferior to the one Stewart Udall did that I am not enclosing either Stew's or mine. I still call "Stew" Mr. Udall to his face, even though I had lunch with him—by accident—in Washington several weeks ago. I am still strong for the stiff arm of reserve against nicknames on sight. Hi, there Whitey! How's the fallout in North Brooklin? About the same here.

Yours ever,
Smitty

5 November 1961

Dear Smitty:

Much has happened since K's appendectomy. In September, after nine months of living with a phantom tumor, she took more tests in New York and the verdict was that she had a block in the carotid artery, right side of the neck. We were ordered to proceed to Rochester, N.Y., for surgery, and we did so, K going into the Strong Memorial Hospital, I into a nearby motel. She was operated on, darn near died (I *did* die), and we are now back home, where instead of getting steadily better she seems to lose a little ground each day and is awfully depressed. I am a wreck and don't write letters to friends anymore because I haven't got it in me, but we hope to pull out of this morass in time. It has been a painful year and a wasted one, as far as any sensible endeavor is concerned. Thanks for your fine letter of 1 November. The only writing I do nowadays is obituary notices, Thurber's being the latest. I'm glad your fall from the roof did no serious damage. A man who puts a porch on a henhouse is, I am afraid, asking for it.

Yrs.,
Whitey

November 26, 1961

Dear Whitey:

Your luck and Katharine's is due for an upgrading, and I hope it is already moving that way in reality, and not just in the Little Theater of my mind.

The thing you did about Thurber was right through the center—". . . he wrote the way a child skips rope, the way a mouse dances," is from diamonds. I read it twice in the *New Yorker* and once in the *Saturday Review*. It lets light through the cloud around death.

You are due a measure of cool reproof for your slurring thrust at one who puts a porch on his henhouse. I put that porch on to give my henhouse distinction. Do you know of any other henhouse which admiring neighbors call "The Chicken Hilton?"

Yours ever,
Smitty
Damariscotta, Maine

January 10, 1962

Dear Whitey:

I don't know whether you are at Fiddlers Bayou, Turtle Bay, or North Brooklin, but wherever you are, I hope you're warm, dry, and in good health. "You" is here used as the plural—i.e., Katharine and EBW.

We are returned to low normal after lying abed with the flu for eight or nine days. The girls occupying the Chicken Hilton are re-flowering after a period of molting, producing enough eggs to again satisfy our pedigreed clientele. The light is thirteen minutes longer than at winter solstice, and there are optimists on Main Street, largely fishermen, who are talking about Spring.

One of your letters describing various hells of surgery and hospitals encountered over the past months stated—or maybe hinted—that you had to get to work to pay the bills. I don't know if you were kidding, or just flinging out a cry to get Fate off your back. In any case, here's something extra special, offered for your consideration.

At my request, my captains at Ford Publications have authorized me to offer you $1,500 (that's fifteen hundred bucks) for 1,200–1,500 words on one of the following subjects, or working titles:

"Days at the Fryeburg Fair"

"How to See A Tree"

"How to Look at a Brook"

"What's for Me in the Sea"

If these don't interest you, we could surely think of others. Something that would take the blinders off the eyes of the highway traveler and enlighten his soul or lift his heart. I want you to know there is no hellish rush. The deadline could be around the middle of April. If you have to say no, I don't want you to feel bad about it. If you say yes, I would hope you'll feel good about it. I sure as hell would. Let me know as soon as convenient. And a Happy New Year to you and K.

Yrs.,
Smitty
Damariscotta, Maine

North Brooklin
11 January 1962

Dear Smitty:

We have been here since returning from Rochester, N.Y.

I can't give you an answer tonight to your fine invitation to write a piece, but will let you know in a few days. I haven't been writing any pieces lately, and don't know that I can. Glad to see, however, that you have got my word rate up over a dollar—very gratifying. Knopf wants me to write an introduction for a forthcoming book and he asked me what I would want for it, and I said I always got 79 cents a word, which was less than Coolidge got, but Coolidge was President. I have Knopf scared now, as he thinks I was in earnest when I said 79 cents. Actually, I can be had dirt cheap, just so long as I can write anything at all, but I like to keep publishers on what a friend of mine used to call tenderhooks.

Yrs.,
Whitey

P.S. I will explain about the staples coming out of the shell and grit box later. It has been on my mind all year and I know exactly what happened.

[Telegram]

Straight Message. Chg. LO 3-3959
Telegram January 13, 1962, E. W. Smith to E. B. White
Mr. E. B. White
North Brooklin, Maine

I am on tenderhooks.

Smitty

North Brooklin
17 January 1962

Dear Smitty:

Thanks for your wire. And thanks for the views of your barn and henhouse and the small, rude bridge that arches an indistinct flood. I sent in my chick order the other day, so spring can't be far behind. I've had my bellyful of Massachusetts Whites and am going back to Silver Cross. Mr. Parmenter failed to send me his literature, and I think he no longer hatches Silvers, so I by-passed him and went on to Wallingford, Connecticut, with my order. My real problem is the fan in my electric brooder stove; the motor is 25 years old, has a tendency to heat up, and I can't find another like it.

If you can wait until the middle of April for a piece, I think I can write one about the sea, but would prefer not to call it, "What's For Me in the Sea." Some time ago I started a piece about the role small boats and the sea had played in my life, and about the problems an aging sailor must face—particularly an aging sailor who habitually sails alone, as is my wont. I set the piece to one side after a bit, and it has lain dormant, while I grew older. If you think this subject fits your requirements, I will tackle it as soon as I get to Fiddlers Bayou, which is an arm of the sea. If the subject sounds repulsive, or unpromising, let me know, and I will sink back into my former condition. We leave here January 31, weather permitting.

Yrs.,
Whitey

P.S. I do not need to earn money any more, as my oldest grandson has a paper route.

January 18, 1962

Dear Whitey:

Yours of yesterday saying you will do the piece on the role small boats and the sea have played in your life got me so far off the tenderhooks that I telephoned my Managing Editor in Dearborn, Robert Martin Hodesh, to report the great news and get glory. Of course, "What's For Me in the Sea" was just an idea-title, and you can call it anything you want that will go through the mails legally. Fiddlers Bayou, I hope, will be a swell place to write it, and I wish I could be with you, except that I would interfere, or bring lime rickeys at over-frequent times. I guess they are the same. My problem, now beginning to loom, is what am I going to do till the middle of April while waiting to read your manuscript. I shall try to face it with fortitude and the long view. Plus the inner faith and knowledge that what's White is right.

Mary and I are much interested in your switch from Massachusetts Whites to Silver Cross. We have been having some doubts about our Parmenter Whites, ever since we got some extra birds, locally, of the same breed. The local Whites, we got thirteen of them for luck, are notably better than the Parmenters in feather, style, comb color, voice, and intellect. Nevertheless, we have considered a switch, too, when the present flock runs out of shell fire. We are thinking of White Rocks, our first love from "The Outermost Henhouse" up at our cabin, or a flock of those black ones with the odd red feathers on the neck. Please advise.

If that motor in your brooder electric stove heats up after twenty-five years, throw it away. It's a fire hazard. Get a new one. What with your grandson's paper route and your *Ford Times* commission, dough is for replenishment of equipment and the soul. There is a relationship here which I can't think through. It has something to do with confidence, but it might trend into arrogance, and so I'm scared of it.

Supplementary report on daylight advance, after my last letter: we are now twenty-six minutes ahead of minimum. Some day they are going to give the Nobel Prize to the *Old Farmer's Almanac*, from which all people get the greatest news on earth, which concerns the going of darkness and the coming of light.

I hope your departure day is clear overhead and under wheel, and that your stay at Fiddlers Bayou won't take you out of state too long. And I thank you for whatever you write, sight unseen, about your life at sea in the lonely shallops. May your grain bill subside, and your birds prosper.

Affectionately,
Smitty

Algonquin Alley
February 8, 1962

Dear Smitty:

Send the recipe for a lime rickey to me. I do not know how to build a lime rickey and do not wish to go ahead blindly.

The trouble with the staples in the shell-and-grit feeder was that in my imagination a hen pen is boarded up and down, with no little 2 × 4 studs, and I sent you, fool fashion, a feeder that must have extended beyond the studs, instead of lying snug up against the wall. This gave your hens a chance to leap up onto the feeder, and subjected the feeder to the unusual strain of a fat hen. The staples pulled out, naturally. No hen has ever leapt up onto my shell and grit feeder, because it is so close to the wall that it offers nothing but discomfort.

I have ordered 75 Buff Cross day-old chicks for April 16 delivery. But the big news about me is that I am creeping up on the Fancy. You probably don't know about the Fancy, and I don't want to get you all heifered up by telling you about it until something definite comes up. . . .

Our train leaves day after tomorrow: the *Silver Meteor*. It orbits Manhattan Transfer three times, then heads straight for Sarasota on a one-track line. Everything hangs on the tensile strength of the cow-catcher.

Yrs.,
Whitey

February 11, 1962

Dear Whitey:

I want you to have the lime rickey formula first thing: In an eight-ounce highball glass, squeeze half a fresh lime. To this, introduce a teaspoonful of simple syrup. Next fold in three ounces of Gordon's or Beefeater gin. (Booth's House of Lord's, if you're feeling theatrical.) Put in all the ice cubes the glass will hold. Fill the interstices in the ice with sparkling water, stir until bubbles rise. Quaff. Two or more of these, and you don't care whether it's a good recipe or not.

Your explanation of the fall of the Shell & Grit Feeder is not entirely satisfactory. We had her pinned flat against the wall—no studs to extend outward. Maybe our shell and grit is heavier than yours. Anyway, it is working swell now.

You left in time to escape another bitter cold spell with cruel winds. Sarasota and the lime rickeys will fix your cold. I remember the *Silver Meteor* well. It once dropped me in a swamp called Nahunta, Georgia, in the frog-croaking dawn of day. There is a no-bell boy hotel there called The Knox. A razorback sow and her eleven young joined me at breakfast in the dining room. I have never been back.

I am deeply pleased and touched that your Buff-cross chicks are arriving April 16. I take this as a clear indication that you are steady-on with your *Ford Times* piece—due the middle of April (or before) which is the 15th. Thus you will feel full of freedom to receive the chicks with a hundred percent attention. You have no idea what a part your small boats are playing in my life.

Have a fine time in the sun, and let me hear how it is down there. We are praying that our wood holds out till the vernal equinox so we can keep the schoolhouse stove fired up in the barn workshop.

Yours,
Smitty
Damariscotta, Maine

North Brooklin
18 February 1962

Dear Smitty:

It is raining here today—quite a novelty to hear water running. Even the mounds of frozen goose dung in my goose pen softened enough so that I could start them with a pickaxe. One of my bantam hens has seen the handwriting on the wall and is starting a nest in a sawed-off nail keg.

I am hard at work trying to construct—I should say reconstruct—the summer of 1923, when I was in Alaska. I didn't have cocktails with the former wife of James Agee, but I did work as firemen's messboy in a ship that got as far north as the ice pack, where, instead of submerging like the *Nautilus*, it just turned around and came back.

Like all sensible Maine people we are going to Florida for March, and will be back just in time to catch the first April blizzard full in the face.

Yrs.,
Whitey

Sarasota, Florida
17 March 1962

Dear Smitty:

I sent a wire, or rather I asked my wife to send one. She and a girl at Western Union cooked up something between them, but knowing what two women are like when they get on the phone together, I would guess that the message went to a Mr. Eddie W. Smits, Stevens-Duryea Company, Sound Bend, Indiana. Katharine thinks all automobiles are Stevens-Duryeas, and I have tried to disabuse her. Anyway, I am very glad you liked the piece, and I would be happy to have the money sent to me here in Sarasota, where I shall be sojourning for another couple of weeks or more.

Would like to know when your *Times* plans to run the piece, and also whether they ever do anything as wild as sending a proof to an author. There is a place where I might want to make a slight fix.

Incidentally, I used the word "pennant" to describe the rope that is part of a mooring, and I am quite sure this is the correct term, but have been able to get no support from Sarasota's dictionaries. Have written my son, who will know, but have not heard a reply yet. He is busy building a new storage shed in his boatyard, and he is an obsessionist like his father—does only one thing to a time.

Weather bad here but is improving. I hope to have a book manuscript ready for the publisher before my chicks arrive in North Brooklin on April 16. Here on Fiddlers Bayou the brooding season is under way—there is a mockingbird on eggs in a cat-proof yucca bush just outside of my window.

Yrs.,
Whitey

March 17, 1962

Dear Whitey:

I received your wire in Dearborn Thursday p.m. shortly before I en-Wolverined for Boston, and so by bus north to Portland and Damariscotta.

The check will go to you at Sarasota, as you instructed, and it usually takes checks about a week to worm their way through the Central Staff Accounting Dept. and get mailed. But they always make it eventually.

In case your ego is for any reason low, here's a couple or so shots for its welfare. I showed "The Sea and the Wind that Blows" to William Shoen, who writes speeches for Henry Ford II, and who also has an eye on our *Ford Times* magazine. Bill read the ms. aloud to his wife, who broke into tears over the emotions engendered by it. Mrs. Shoen is a writer herself, and Bill reports that she asked, after drying her eyes: "Do you suppose E. B. White just wrote this right off? Is this his first draft?" So I told Bill to tell her, to ease her mind: "Not exactly a first draft. He's been working on this for forty years."

I also, with pride, placed a copy of the piece on the desk of the Secretary to Theodore H. Mecke, Jr., General Public Relations Manager of the Ford Motor Company. Mr. Mecke is so high up in the company I don't even know him by sight, let alone he me. But everyone who knows him admires him, and from afar I am fond of him, because he is an admirer of you and your work. I couldn't be more pleased by anything than by the letter from him which I received this morning here at home. It goes like this, verbatim:

Dear Mr. Smith:

The White piece is a thing of beauty, Thank you for sharing it with me and for making it possible for a rarity like this to appear in the *Ford Times*.
Sincerely,
Ted Mecke

So you see, Whitey, you made a lot of people better people. Thanks again. And best to you and Katharine.

Yours,
Smitty

P.S. The big storm of last Tuesday blew four rails off of my back fence, and the birds celebrated by laying 26 eggs according to Mary's precise production charts.

P.P.S. Snow wasting fast in warm sun and still airs.

March 22, 1962

Dear Whitey:

Yours of the 17th has been carefully read by me and by our Nautical Department, which consists of Edward Myers and Dwight Tracy. You are all clear and correct in your use of the word "pennant" in your piece for *Ford Times* about the sea. In fact, the Nautical Department gave a resounding okay to the other 1,413 words in the story. I think they want to make a Joseph Conrad out of you.

I told the boys you were also good on Whip-poor-Willie and showed them an advance copy of April's *Field & Stream* to prove it. This issue of *F. & S.* should be on the newsstands at about the time you get this letter. On page 35, there's a story by me, but the first paragraph is by you, in quotes—your description of the dark bird, which you kindly gave me permission to use.

Your "Seas and the Wind That Blows" hasn't been scheduled as yet, but I will keep you informed. I talked to my boss, C. H. Dykeman, on the phone yesterday p.m., and he agrees that you will see proofs on the piece, and that no editing of any sort will be done except by you. He is a guy with understanding in these matters, and he feels warmly favorable to writers who like to follow their stuff right through to press time. It shows they take an interest in their work. So you'll have ample chance for the fix, if you want a fix; and if space requirements call for cutting a line or two or maybe adding one, the scalpel is in your hands.

No mockingbirds or yucca bushes outside my window: but the birds in the Chicken Hilton are laying splendid eggs and seem to be talking of spring. The cover of my well is now visible as the snow dies away, and there are warm bare spots under the cedars. It's damn near time you were coming home.

Tell me about your new book, Whitey. I'm all agog, and so is the Nautical Department. Best to Katharine and the Western Union girl. Their wire came through fine.

Yours ever,
Smitty
Damariscotta, Maine

March 28, 1962

Dear Smitty:

This will have to be a quick one, as three pretty girls are waiting for me to take them swimming. My thanks for the check, which arrived and is too big for so slight a contribution. I don't intend to tell Ford how to run his business, though. I would feel like the bat boy of the Chicago White Sox who sidled up to Al Lopez the other day during an inning when the Sox were being walloped all over the place, and said, "Mr. Lopez, don't you think you'd better take that pitcher out?" "Zip it up, kid," replied. Mr. Lopez. "You're the bat boy, I'm the manager—let's keep it that way."

Am tracking down a copy of *Field & Stream* and expect to meet with success today. Look forward to reading your piece.

My son says "pennant" is it. I'm glad there is no quarrel between him and your Nautical Department. I'll tell you about my new book when I get good and ready—it's the oldest story ever told.

And now for the sea and Beauty.

Yrs.,
Whitey

March 29, 1962

Dear Whitey:

Wild geese go thundering over our house in hourly flocks of about 174. It "unhinges the mind" and releases the soul. First robin group arrived today. The porch on the Chicken Hilton hove, but is now settled again as the frost leaves. Hornets are coming out of their winter daze.

I thought I knew all about procrastination, but a new wrinkle is to read the enclosed stuff by David McCord, which he recently sent me. I have read it two mornings in a row and then quit work. "In Sight of Sever" mentions your name along with a couple other guys you may of heard of.

In sending me the enclosed things, Dave writes: "Did I ever tell you [me] that I came across, in an old bound copy of *St. Nicholas,* a piece of prose that looked startlingly familiar? After I had read it, I glanced down and saw that it was signed Elwyn Brooks White. The style was implicit from the beginning."

Did your check come from Dearborn okay?

Please tell what your new book is about. I could hardly stir up a respectable advance sale in this vicinity.

Yrs.,
Smitty
Damariscotta, Maine

Sarasota, Fla.
April 6, 1962

Dear Smitty:

Too busy to write. I can remember when the South was lazy, sultry, and relaxed. Now it is all hooked up and there is not a minute to be lost.

Am returning the David McCord pieces, with thanks. Just heard that on 6 May, when Thoreau is admitted to the Hall of Fame, three of the guests will be Nehru, Justice Douglas, and Secretary Udall. I won't go unless there is woodchuck on the menu.

Enjoyed your fishing yarn in *Field & Stream* and trembled all over at learning that a man had once hooked an otter. I've only tangled once with an otter, and I was very glad she didn't have a fish hook in her. She didn't like me even *without* a fish hook.

We leave here Monday, and if nothing happens, we will arrive home the 16th.

Yrs.,
Whitey

April 23, 1962

Dear Whitey:

Over to the Farnsworth Museum the other day to look at some Andrew Wyeth watercolors, figuring they might be used in the *Ford Times* with your sea story. But the ones I saw, though marvelous, showed no sail, and your piece calls for sail, it seems to me. While at the museum, whom do I run into by chance but Andrew Wyeth's father-in-law, a Mr. James. And this man told me how you and Mr. Wyeth (whom I have never met) got your honorary degrees at Colby under the same blanket. It was an amusing story. Armed with it, plus the approval of our Art Director, I sent your story to Andrew Wyeth imploring him to get on the ball and illustrate it. Jeese, will I be glad if he does! If he can't do some originals, I think he might let us reproduce one of his paintings showing some sail. (He let us use his "Kelp Ledge" with a dory story in our March Issue.)

What about Thoreau and the Hall of Fame, which you mentioned in yours of 6 April? Dave McCord and I are both mystified. Were you kidding, or is it really something? If so, I could get a woodchuck for the menu. I feel in the mood, and qualified, since I have just finished a piece on outdoor etiquette called, "Into the Woods with Emily Post."

Your snootiness in withholding dope on the subject of your new book is raising hell with you around here. Here's the way the conversations go:

Person: Is it true E. B. White's having a new book?
Smitty: That's what he says.
Person: What's it about?
Smitty: It's a mystery.
Person: Mr. White writing a whodunnit?

Smitty: Yeah.

Person: Why?

Smitty: He's broke—Florida dog tracks.

So you better tell all.

I'm enclosing a semi-privately published pamphlet by Dave McCord, and don't ask me what semi-privately means. I always thought he was a good writer, and now I'm sure of it. Just run your eye over the boys mentioned on page 19—and then please return in the stamped envelope, also enclosed.

Did your birds arrive okay? Did *you*?

Best to you and Katharine,
Smitty
Damariscotta, Maine

N. Brooklin
26 April 1962

Dear Smitty:

Have just read David McCord's address to the overseers, enjoyed
it, and think it is full of fine emotion and some pretty good
words, too, like "gnathic," which I haven't had time to look up
yet. I feel the same way about New England but haven't got
about in it the way McCord has, haven't climbed the mountains
or been on the rivers, and so I am made to feel like a stick-in-the-
mud by this piece, which I am. I didn't know you could catch a
frog with a Black-eyed Susan.

My day-old chicks arrived in excellent shape by mail from
Wallingford. They are doing well—better than I am. My book,
about which you inquired, is just a clip book of my Letter pieces.
Am trying to write short postscripts to the pieces in an attempt
to remove the coating of dust that has settled on them. Two
ducks spent yesterday on my frog pond, in the snow.

Yrs.,
Whitey

May 7, 1962
Monday Morn

Dear Smitty:

There is a chance that I might like to use my Sea piece as the windup item in my forthcoming book. Do you know when the *Times* plans to bring it out, and is there a way I can get a proof of it or a copy of it right away? Would Ford permit me to use it, assuming of course that the *Times* publication date comes before my book publication date?

I can't recall whether or not I explained this book to you. It is a collection of my Letter pieces that appeared in the *New Yorker*, plus a piece on *Walden* that was published in the *Yale Review* in 1954 on the hundredth anniversary. I'm writing postscripts to these letters, trying to bring them up to date. The sea piece would make a satisfactory postscript to the last piece in the book, which is about my sea voyage to Alaska in the summer of 1923.

My manuscript is due at Harpers on May 15, so any information or advice you can give me would be greatly appreciated by

Yrs. in the coils,
Whitey

May 8, 1962

Dear Whitey:

The boys in Dearborn report that "The Sea" is not scheduled till May, 1963. This means it can't come out in the book—if the book is for October publication, this year. I'm sorry about this. And I hope you are not going to be too disappointed. Anyway, you'll have "The Sea," for your *next* book

Still no word from Andrew Wyeth. Do you have anyone in mind you would like to do sketches for the piece? Our Art Director says he would welcome suggestions.

Yours,
Smitty
Damariscotta, Maine

May 8, 1962

Dear Whitey:

Here's "The Sea," as promised over the phone just now. And it was nice to talk to you about these affairs of the literary. I hope it will work out so you use it in the book; and in any case, l shall try to persuade the boys to run the piece in September or October of this year, which would seem to clear it as far as publication dates are concerned.

I'll call the office tomorrow on this, and let you know what the decision is on dates, if any. By the way, if we can't get Andrew Wyeth to illustrate "The Sea," have you any suggestions?

Yours,
Smitty
Damariscotta, Maine

P.S. Our Pencil Pecking Dept. gave you a check on the spelling of "stationary."

North Brooklin
June 4, 1962

Dear Smitty:

I've owed you a letter for a long time but I've been pooched. Thanks for sending me the copy of the sea piece. I'm not very disappointed about its not being in the book, as I had not really planned to use a postscript to the Alaska piece—which is the last piece in the book and ends in a way that makes a suitable windup.

About an illustrator, I have no idea, nobody in mind. I'd better leave this to you.

I started 77 day-old Silver Cross chicks (from Hall Brothers, Wallingford, Conn.) about six weeks ago, and they are now all feathered out and very pretty to look at. One day when they were about three weeks old, one of them got the taste of blood and suddenly cannibalism was in full swing. Luckily, I happened to look in on them. Four birds were bleeding, but not bad. I caught all four, applied pine tar to the wounds, nailed blankets over the windows, inserted a red light bulb into the socket, and things quieted down for a spell. Next day I put two big turves into their outdoor run, and it is amazing how the birds went for them. They not only ate the grass and the weeds, they picked the turves to pieces, ate all the earthworms and then the earth itself. Chickens in confinement are in need of dirt in their diet, in my opinion. I was afraid for a while I was going to have a neighbor come and de-beak my birds, but with any luck, I plan to win through without this mutilating surgery. I don't care for the looks of a de-beaked bird.

Have just sent away to a man in Michigan ordering 12 Fawn Runner duck eggs. I have a broody hen in the barn, and this morning is the kind of morning a man takes a look around at sea and woods, field and sky, and sits down and gets off a letter to Michigan ordering a few duck eggs to slip under a quiet hen.

The mail has just come, bringing newsbreaks to be processed by the oldest living newsbreak processor, so must say good-bye. Any time you want a Fawn Runner duckling, let me know.

Yrs.,
Whitey

July 2, 1962

Dear Whitey:

The Colby College people, sponsors for some part of your academic standing, have asked me to give them the original of your ms., "The Sea and the Wind That Blows." They want to have your rubrics* lying or hanging around there in the hallowed halls to show how good they are in conferring degrees, especially since next year is their sesquicentennial, when they are going whole hog for Maine art, artists, writers, and characters. To have "The Sea" under lights, preferably non-neon, is fine by me and my Ford connections. Of course I would have some fun making marginal notes in my own fair hand on this sheaf of yellow pages, but would desist out of reticence. (When was Smitty reticent?) Could you give me an affirmative on this soon?

The beautiful Julia (Meyers), one of our pedigreed egg customers (Jumbos at all times), reported your secret trip through Damariscotta the other day. I was at first infuriated that you didn't come down to see the Chicken Hilton, then realized that you were jealous—or else zeroing in for home. On either count, you are forgiven.

David McCord is today back from the West Coast. I'll be hearing from him soon about his promised visit to me, Henry Beston, and you. If we call on you, it will only set you back a few days in Life's Plan. Lay in a small stock of Gordon's Gin & Coke against the evil day. Are the Balm of Gileads still standing? I use landmarks instead of route signs, and what with the road developments, it gets me into lots of trouble. The landmarks disappear. So does your good and faithful friend.

Smitty
Damariscotta, Maine

Smitty's definition of rubrics is anything penciled in by the author, any time, any place, anywhere.

North Brooklin
July 1962

Dear Smitty (if I may call you that):

Andy is quite sick and he has asked me to get a note off to you today. He is struggling to get his book proofs off this week and then must go into the local hospital for tests, so, much as we would like to see you and David McCord here, it won't be possible for us just now.

He also wants me to explain that because he has deeded to the Cornell Library all his manuscripts, he cannot let the original manuscript of "The Sea and the Wind That Blows" go to Colby. Already a part of his manuscripts and correspondence is at Cornell, and the rest is to follow as he gets time to prepare it. Please just return the manuscript to Andy when the *Ford Times* can part with it. No hurry, of course.

We would have stopped to see you on our way through last week if we did not have to press on as fast as possible, if only because Henry Allen, who works for us, had to get home. He met us with our car at the train station outside of Boston (Route 128). Andy was not well enough to drive the car himself; at least not all the way.

In haste,
Katharine (S.W.)

P.S. Andy is going to the hospital today. Couldn't finish his proofs.

July 6, 1962

Dear Katharine:

Why do nice guys have to get sick—especially the very nice ones, like Whitey? I hope it's something the doctors can fix soon, and that he'll be up and at the proofs again.

Tell him to rest easy about "The Sea" manuscript and also the threatened visit by Dave McCord and me. I'll divert the ms. to Andy, and explain the matter to the Colby people.

I'll also divert McCord and myself.

Give Andy my affectionate regards, and tell him not to worry about anything but getting well.

Sincerely,
Smitty
Damariscotta, Maine

Saturday, Oct. 20, 1962

Dear Whitey:

What the hell happened? Last word was from Katharine in July reporting you in hospital and feeling too lousy to work on your proofs. I hope you're well again.

We had a fine summer, Mary's garden supplying lettuce to Gay's fancy grocery and Saltwater Farm Pier, and enough canoe trips in the north country to keep me well supplied with lame backs, which I cured playing golf.

My really big news is a letter from my ex-wife, whom I haven't seen in fifteen years. She's teaching college freshmen in English Composition and asked me to tell her the title of the best book for shaping up their literary efforts. I wrote her to get hold of *Elements of Style* and her English Department has now ordered forty (40) copies. This goes to show that one author's divorce helps feather another author's nest.

Our flock in the Chicken Hilton is motley. One day my wife went off in the car to find someone who would butcher and process our Massachusetts Whites. She came back with six Rhode Island Red laying pullets, and on another expedition brought back a dozen coal black layers. They worked in so well with the others we called them the "Peace Corps."

What's your book news? Write.

Smitty

P.S. I am gradually leaking out of the more arduous Dearborn editorial duties. Last word I had on your piece about the sea was that Ed Turner had done the illustrations and they were planning to run the piece in a June issue. Seems like when the boys out there get hold of a good thing they want to hang onto it forever. Sm'ty

Sunday, Oct. 21, 1962

Dear Whitey:

One of the questions in my recent note—the one about the book—is answered in the *NY Times*'s full-paper of today. If the picture means anything, and I hope it does, the question of your health is also answered. I never saw you looking so good. Whitey boy, you're benign! (I'm speaking of the picture.)

Cheers from Smitty and probably a lot of other characters.

Yrs.,
Smitty

Sunday, Nov. 11, 1962

Dear Whitey:

What you wrote in the book ("been having poor run of luck") has a brooding note. It sounds like John Oakhurst, gambler, of Poker Flat, but I hope it isn't that bad.

The Points of My Compass is a full wallet. I'd read most of them in the *New Yorker*, and was glad to find my piece of beaver wood between hard covers at last. That beaver, wherever he is, rates high in the species. But when I got aboard the Buford, Skagway bound, I was really sailing. I haven't enjoyed a piece so much in ages. The thing is not only good for its own sake, but for mine. I was running parallel with you on the East Coast—fired from the *Boston American* in 1923, while you were being fired, simultaneously probably, from the *Seattle Times*. I note that we both were reading *Faint Perfume* and Hatrack in the *A. Mercury*, and probably Erik Dorn. I, too, was a Morley man, and trending into Sherwood Anderson, with already a large collection of speakeasy cards. "Years of Wonder" makes them wonderful years again—but with pain now buried beneath layers of scar tissue. Your book stands out for another very special reason. It's the only one I've come across that was a jacket on which I believe every word.

Thanks to beat hell.

Yrs.,
Smitty
Damariscotta, Maine

North Brooklin
December 7, 1962

Dear Smitty:

. . . I sold my sloop last summer. That piece I wrote is going to sound a bit queer when it emerges in print, but most people will not notice that anything is amiss. I wrote it under the impression that it would be published last spring. There is not much news to report. My 25 Silver Cross pullets hit a high of 23 eggs twice recently, and they are the prettiest birds I ever mothered. I also have a pen of fancy birds—Partridge Plymouth Rocks, four hens and a rooster. Raised 'em from eggs that I bought from a Harvard man named Allen, who lives in Maine, operates a motel, and indulges himself in the fancy. My son has had a fine year with his boatyard, business up fifty percent, goodwill up a hundred percent, and a big new storage shed just completed.

Hope all is well with you and that you will enjoy a happy festive season. Time to cut a few young fir trees and stick them in the ground close to your kitchen door, before freeze-up. Place a stale doughnut on the tip of one of the trees, and you will have more chickadees than you can count on both of your six-toed feet.

Yrs.,
Whitey

December 25, 1962
Christmas

Dear Whitey:

I hope that artery in Katharine's leg has the good grace to find a bypass, or will re-canalize as I have heard it called. Let there be an end to anxiety and pain. This is written with special vehemence and no idle sympathy, since I have just had a siege of both—anxiety and pain, that is. A four-hour operation on my right hand ten days ago for a *Dupuytrens contracture*, to you a curling and stiffening of the fingers. (I call it "Lon Chaney Hand.") It went fine, except that four days after, I got a gout attack in the ankle—first in years. I didn't think it was fair, but the croakers say gout is a sequel to the upset of an operation—if you have ever had gout. So tell K, I know what an ankle pain is like, and to hell with it.

This is my first day out of bed, and I have a boxing glove sized bandage on my pinkies, so that writing to you is a Spartan effort. I haven't had a drink or a keyboard at hand for two weeks, and my one bright Christmas thought was for a cartoon from Charles Addams of a Christmas morning scene in The House, where that awful little boy is towing by a string his three favorite presents, all mounted on wheels—a guillotine, a gallows, and an electric chair. (If C. A. hasn't done it before, he ought to.)

I've read several reviews of *Compass*, notably the ones in the *Wall Street Journal*, and *Saturday Review*. One of these—in *SR*; I think—attempted to analyze White, and found it rough going. I was glad. This type of analysis strikes me as prying, or privacy-violating, and to the critic you went up in smoke anyway—"elusive," I think he called you, referring to your work. Whitey, when you're elusive, you're really in. Let me be in the forefront with congratulations. I don't have to warn you to stay elusive. No one is going to catch you, anyway.

In substantiation of this thought, I enclose a review of *Compass* that was my last act of writing before I left for the gas chamber in Portland Medical Center. I was sure at the time that it was my last act of any kind.

Good news about your birds and your son's boatyard. Our friend (and yours), Ed Myers, was up to your son's yard while cruising with someone last summer. Ed had good things to say about it.

Can't see where your selling the sloop will in any way affect "Sea and the Wind That Blows." I can't wait to see the piece in type. Should think galleys should be along soon. What's your address in Florida? That's important. If any of the young beavers out there starts cutting your stuff just to make a page even, I want to be in touch with you so you can do it yourself. You have it in writing that that's the way it's to be.

Let me know all.

Health and happiness to you both.

Smitty

Sarasota

Jan. 3, 1963

Sorry, very sorry to learn of your troubles. Will write when I get shed of a few of my own. News of K is good. Warm air is very beneficial.

Whitey

On a hand-written postcard of a palm tree.

Sarasota, Florida
3 February 1963

Dear Smitty

I was saddened to learn of your troubles and hope you are well out of them by now. Curiously enough, the Lon Chaney hand was described to Katharine and me by our New York doctor just a few hours before your letter arrived. I'd never heard of it before. It was a name that means the position of a doctor's hand as he is about to receive the head of a baby as it is being born. . . .

I want to thank you for sending me the review, and even more for writing it. I was very pleased to be so well spoken of by you in the public prints. My publisher writes that the book is doing well, for which I am thankful, but what I'm waiting for now is for the *author* to do well. The ulcer diet doesn't bother me too much as I don't pay a great deal of attention to it and decided instantly that I wouldn't quit drinking, no matter what the directions said. I have quit coffee, tea, tobacco, and television, but I never cared particularly for any of those things.

The weather hasn't been bad, and the warmth has helped K's circulation. So I am hopeful that I'll not have to pull out of here.

Yrs.,
Whitey

February 15, 1963

Dear Whitey:

My relief on learning that you have not quit drinking, but just quit tea, coffee, tobacco, and television, has inspired the following formula for the economy of life:

If your liquor bills exceed your food bills, you're drinking too much. If your food bills exceed your liquor bills, you're eating too much.

That's a hell of a note about your ulcer. I am no good on anxiety, either, unless I take a firm hand. I once wrote—compiled, rather—a play with three titles: *The Fall of the House of Ulcer*, *Moon over Miasma,* and *Gray's Anatomy in a Country Churchyard.* In brief, the play told how Lady Catheter's daughter Hernia was wooed and won by a dashing cavalry officer, Major Duodenum. After a lot of grief, they were finally married by the Reverend Gonad to the strains of the Ovarian Rhapsody played on the Fallopian tuba. One of the harrowing side effects of your ulcer is that it reminded me of this and I hope you will forgive me.

My "Lon Chaney" hand (or *Dupuytrens contracture*) is a lot better. A good thing, too, because I need every cord and fiber in shape for snow shoveling. Stay right there in Fiddler's Bayou, Whitey. This has been and is being one of the bitterest winters in a long time—icy roads, snow, gale winds, and zero and below temperatures. It's been going on for two months, almost, with scarcely a break. We are all full of aches and pains, and we don't know whether it's the snow shovel or the weather. The birds in the Chicken Hilton seem to love it. Their plumage is thick and prosperous looking, their eggs clean and huge. They all crowd into the open doorway to take the afternoon sun, the black, whites, and mulattoes smoothly integrated.

The automation on your x-ray group and tooth extractioners goes right along with the enclosed clipping Ed Meyers left in our mailbox. This is something you have excoriated in the past in writing. Note the type-line partly torn at the bottom of the clipping. Pretty frightening, if I read it right. "Gassed Roses." Jesus.

Glad you liked the review about *The Points of My Compass*. Comments on the book all around here are full of warmth and admiration—just the stuff to knock the hell out of an ulcer.

I've recently finished a piece for *Field & Stream* on stillness. It centers around Kidney Pond Camps in the mountains of Baxter Park, easily accessible by car. No motors allowed—outboard, inboard, or pontoon plane. You paddle your own canoe. What is more silent than a canoe under paddle? The place is clean, comfortable, and well managed. I think you and Katharine would like it for a few days of quality solitude—lots of quiet little ponds, mountains climbing right out of them. If you ever get the urge, I'll tell you more.

I have also written a brief epic of vituperation against the mannerisms which infect our daily conversation like a verbal pox. Things like "I mean," "You know," "What I mean," "But I mean, after *all*," "My point is," "Let me put it this way," "In my opinion," "Let me finish," "In other words," "Frankly," "Candidly," and "To be honest with you." And a lot more. My agent (Brandt & Brandt) is enthusiastic—and I await a large check anxiously.

Good, better, and best health to you and K. And a murrain on The House of Ulcer. The same goes for the gassed roses.

Yrs.,
Smitty
Damariscotta, Maine

Sarasota

Feb. 23, 1963

Quickest way to destroy stillness is to write a piece about it, giving the location. People will swarm there to see what you are talking about, many of them armed with cap pistols and transistor radios. Fair warning!

Whitey

On a hand-written postcard of a tropical Florida scene.

Fiddler Bayou
29 March 1963

Dear Smitty:

I have our reservations on the *Meteor* for the 23rd of April. I chose that date because of "twenty-three skidoo"—an expression that is vintage with me and you and very helpful at times.

Thanks for the clipping—or as the British say "cutting"— from *The Observer*. Luckily I don't believe half of what I read, let alone what the crazy English write.

Your man Palme out in Never Never Land, Michigan, dropped the sentence from my sea piece about Humphrey Bogart's funeral. What's the matter with you guys—scared of a casket? I am considering *not* buying a Ford when I get back home, if I ever do. That'll learn you.

If you've had only three Canada geese you are being short-changed in South Bristol. I received a letter from my daughter-in-law this morning, and she reports twenty-one geese in Brooklin near the boatyard. Here on Fiddler Bayou we have a pair of mourning doves building in the Cunningham pine, a pair of mockers building in the yucca right next to where I do my drinking (to cure my ulcer), and redwings scouting the mangroves. We also have an injured shag. It was found on the boulevard, on the center stripe, tended by a neighbor's beagle puppy and another neighborhood dog named Rusty, who spends all his time with us because he knows class when he sees it. The beagle puppy had been run over in the same spot just a few days ago, but was right back on the center stripe to see about a shag.

Life here is sub-marginal at the moment as we are enjoying a plague of dead fish. Some people say they are victims of the Red Tide, others that they are victims of the sinking of the *Sulphur*

Queen, a freighter that went down in the Gulf with a cargo of molten sulphur. All I know for sure is that there is a hell of a stink around the shores, including my swimming hole at the mouth of the Bayou. The gulls won't touch the corpses either. They probably know what they are doing. But the sand crabs eat them, and at the entrance to every crab burrow you find the picked bones of a fish. Trouble is, there aren't enough crabs.

Thanks again for the clipping.

Yrs.,
Whitey

April 13, 1963

Dear Whitey:

As of your letter of the 29 March, the Ford Motor Company owes you two "son-of-a-bitches" and one casket shaped like a boat. The son-of-a-bitches were eliminated one each from our reprints of your "Farewell, My Lovely!" Bogey's casket was snatched from your "Sea and the Wind That Blows." I envision a little scene where Bogey's ghost drifts into the *Ford Times* office and stops at Jerry Palme's desk. Bogey is carrying a Thompson gun with practiced ease, and he has a couple of "the boys" with him. He is about to administer punishment to our Jerry, when he notices Jerry's lovely secretary. So he nods to the boys, and indicating our Jerry with a muzzle gesture from the Thompson, says:

"Take the bastid out and shoot him. I want to be alone with the dame."

What with all this anti-casket, anti-s.o.b. stuff, you may think we have been taken over by the *Christian Science Monitor*. But no. The only way I can figure it is that Henry Ford II found out you had bought a Lark and is trying to get even. Actually, I don't know how, or why, the casket got lost; and I hope you are not sore at me and will go right out and buy a Model T.

I rejoice to hear that you will be aboard the *Meteor* on Twenty-Three Skidoo day of this month. You are timing it just right, if today is a sample of the weather you'll come back to. Snow about gone, and our fields showing an omen of green. Redwings back in force, and our osprey caught its first mole in the upper piece yesterday. Don't tell me ospreys don't catch moles. Ours has been doing it for the eight years we've been here—a marvelous, shallow glide, undercarriage down, to scoop up the mole, and aloft again. A lovely, predatory operation.

It is good to think you'll soon be curing your ulcer on your own, three-million-dollar terrace. I must sign off, now, as I have to build a bridge—Smitty's Two-by-Four Cantilever Model, Mark Two.

Yours,
Smitty
Damariscotta, Maine

May 21, 1963

Dear Whitey:

Did you make it home okay aboard the *Meteor* on Skidoo Day?

Your "Sea & Wind" story in June *Ford Times* looks and reads swell. Did the boys send you some copies? I have a few spares if you need any. You are a very fine writer.

Oh, you kid!

Smitty

31 May 1963

Dear Smitty:

I don't need any spare copies, all I need is my sloop, which is gone. The artist gave me a perfectly wonderful sloop, and I am crazy about it, but it is very hard to handle alone.

We made it home, after I had an unexpected operation, which seemed to involve the removal of quite a bit of jawbone. I don't really miss it much, but driving Route 128 the day following the procedure was wracking to my nervous system, which is no good anyway.

I am not going to write for the *Ford Times* anymore, on account of the way they took Humphrey Bogart away from me. I quit the *Seattle Times* in spirit when they disallowed me the use of certain words, but they got the jump on me and fired me—I would have quit sooner or later. I don't fool around. Am not nasty or surly, just firm.

I have a broody hen on 10 Partridge Plymouth Rock eggs, also have 76 Silver Cross chickens, six weeks old today, also 25 old Silver hens laying 80 percent. But the big news is, I have a pair of bluebirds. They took over a nesting box that has been occupied by tree swallows for ten days. I saw the takeover and it was magnificent. A battle royal, right down in the dirt of the driveway and into the barn on the north side. No holds barred. I've been waiting for this for almost thirty years. So have the tree swallows, I guess.

Yrs.,
Whitey

July 6, 1963

Dear Whitey:

The news of your latest and greatest award* reached me over the phone the other morning via the delighted voice of our mutual friend Ed Meyers. I am just as delighted as Ed, and so is everyone I talk to. It's no-kidding wonderful to hear, and all us experts are as one in saying you deserve the honor, whether you think so or not. And whatever you think, you must be feeling fine.

One of the pleasing things about your honor is that it gives me the perfect excuse to send you the enclosed piece, which appears in the current (July) *Redbook* under a different title, one they dreamed up. They also eliminated a couple of "Humphrey Bogarts," so I am sending you the pure Smitty. I figure when you get down there in the White House, President Kennedy or Caroline or someone will ask you to stand up and make a speech. (If Frank Sinatra asks you to sing, don't do it.) My piece, enclosed, will help your speech, since it tells you exactly what not to say. If you say practically anything except what I recommend for oblivion, you will come out okay—and maybe get another medal to boot.

I play golf every Saturday morning in a five-some consisting of four men and a Dachshund, a female whose name was Jeanie until her owner, Ken Colby, read *The Points of My Compass*. She is now called Fred. She lies down between the ball and the hole when you are putting, and is usually in line with your backswing as you drive off any tee. She eats divots, and some of mine are larger than otter pelts. She loves casual water on hot days. On cold days she crawls into your golf bag. Fred to the core. Your far-reaching influence, or Fred's?

My latest wrinkle in procrastination is making lettuce deliveries for Mary's abundant garden business. Saltwater Pier, two trips a day; Gay's Fancy Grocery, two a day. Some days it totals as much as twenty-eight bucks. Gin, golf balls, and a useful circumventing of the typewriter. I dread the very shadow of winter.

There was a murder in the Chicken Hilton night before last. The FBI says coon. How are your birds doing? How are you and K. doing?

Affection and admiration and congratulations to the both of you.

As ever,
Smitty
Damariscotta, Maine

E. B. White was chosen for the Presidential Medal of Freedom by President John F. Kennedy.

New York
July 15, 1963

Dear Smitty:

Excuse ballpoint. Hotels no longer provide ink for their guests.
    I liked your piece about cleaning up the language. You forgot the word "actually." I know a woman who begins almost every sentence with "Actually." It gives even the most fragile thought or message a lot of spurious import.

Yrs.,
Whitey

February 28, 1964

Dear Whitey:

The last time I saw you was in October at Marion Village. You and K. were both looking fine, your Hutchinson Freckle and all. Then at Christmas we had your card, a gay report on the placement of the nature-faking robin, with the chickadees giving it the go-by, or snoot. Now, a short while ago, a wheel from the International Paper Company stopped at our house because he knows some of our relatives. His name is Phil Sargent, and he was born in Sedgwick, Maine. He said he had heard you were ailing, and I am writing to express the hope that he was misinformed.

We are just back from a motor trip to Sea Island, Georgia, which my wife calls the most expensive playpen in the world. The owner's brother was my roommate at Antioch, which explains how we could afford it. The trip was our first non-business one in years, and we managed to stay away from home for thirteen days. Quite a triumph. The boys uptown were laying even money we would turn back before crossing the Kittery-Portsmouth bridge. It was a driving experience. In the ten years plus since we have done any distance touring, roads, speeds, and signs have all changed. I figure we had about eight hundred narrow escapes, including two in the Baltimore Tunnel—one each way. The bridges and the pikes themselves are engineering marvels. But the pace is too fast for Smitty.

The Chicken Hilton has been vacant for several months, but we are about to populate it with thirty-six near-laying pullets soon. Just ordinary Harco blacks for egg production, the English sparrow of the poultry world.

Did you write anything in the *New Yorker* about Kennedy's death that I might have missed? If so, could you tell me the date of issue?

You and K. are probably in Sarasota on the Bayou. A good thing, too. It was zero here early this morning. I hope the report of your illness was a phony. Let me know.

Yours,
Smitty
Damariscotta, Maine

3 March 1964

Dear Smitty:

I'm not ailing (or not much, anyway) but Katharine has been having an awful time with a mysterious skin eruption. She landed in Harkness in January, and stayed there two weeks while the dermatologists held court over her. Things got a little better, and we packed off to the bayou. K has had so many troubles during the last three years it seems unfair that she has to slug this one out; but she has any amount of courage—I would have been dead by this time.

While we were in Sarasota, friends of ours named Roy and Helen Barrette, of Brooklin, dropped by on their way from Mexico to Sea Island. Maybe you encountered them whilst at the playpen. I don't think I would last long at Sea Island, as I only have one pair of trousers. And I feel the way you do about modern highway travel—the pace is all wrong, and the thought of it scares me.

Got to scamper now, as I have to get to Gristede's before sundown, to get my milk. I will send you the paragraph on Kennedy.

More later,
Whitey

Fri., March 6, 1964

Smitty:

This is all I wrote for the *New Yorker*. It was reprinted quite widely and is the closing paragraph in the book *Four Days* (Heritage Press).

Katherine getting worse and I'm getting scared, who scares easy.

Yrs. in haste and desolation,
Whitey

John F. Kennedy
When we think of him, he is without a hat, standing in the wind and the weather. He was impatient of topcoats and hats, preferring to be exposed, and he was young enough and tough enough to confront and enjoy the cold and the wind of these times, whether the winds of nature or the winds of political circumstance and national danger. He died of exposure, but in a way that he would have settled for—in the line of duty, and with his friends and enemies all around, supporting him and shooting at him. It can be said of him, as of few men in a like position, that he did not fear the weather, and did not trim his sails, but instead challenged the wind itself, to improve its direction and to cause it to blow more softly and more kindly over the world and its people.

Sunday, March 8, 1964

Dear Whitey:

We are pulling hard for K. and you, and hope your scare is a gone thing by the time this reaches you, or better yet, before. Thanks for taking time out to send the paragraph on Kennedy. I don't wonder it has been widely reprinted, or that it is the last word in the Heritage Press's *Four Days*. You said it for me. You kept the young man on earth and in the sky and wind at the same time. It's right, and true, and it comes clear though the fell creep of eulogy.

May you both be basking on the North Brooklin terrace soon.

Yours,
Smitty
Damariscotta, Maine

May 7, 1964

Dear Whitey:

The Chicken Hilton group of twenty-five Black Cross birds is making sensational scores—21, 22, 20, 23, 21, and today, 24! Refined clients are flocking in for these fruits of the womb, and my pocket jingles with silver—which eventually finds its way back to Mr. Wirthmore.

What is the news about Katharine? I hope she is back with you at the farm by the sea, all recovered from things reported in your last letter. We have been thinking of you. A lot of people do.

I have a semi-fiction piece in the current (May) issue of *Field & Stream*. I expect you to rush out and buy a copy, because it has a drinking scene in which you would have been welcome.

Holt, Winston & Rinehart told me over the phone yesterday that they are bringing out a book by me—a collection of essays and narratives. I haven't seen the papers yet, but they didn't sound as though they were kidding. Besides, I think I owe you a book—the payoff for *Elements of Style*.

Let me know how you are, Whitey. Okay?

Yours,
Smitty
Damariscotta, Maine

North Brooklin
May 22, 1964

Dear Smitty:

. . . Your pride in the egg-laying prowess of these ready-made pullets is beyond comprehension to a man who rears his own chicks in springtime and who won't see the first pullet egg until the September morning when he finds one on the range. But every man to his own excess. And this reminds me I still haven't delivered the handsome White automatic two-pail sanitary waterer that I so kindly built for you a couple of years ago. Everything in good time.

Glad to hear you are going to have a book out. I've had my last book; nineteen is enough books and I'm tired. I read that tall tale of yours in *Field & Stream* and I envy you having such a whacky father-in-law. The part I liked best was when the saw went *shish shish*, a sound I miss around here nowadays, where saws go *Brrt-waaa waaaaaaa*. The only *shish shishing* is when I go out myself and prune the deadwood off my lovely old diseased apple trees. Last week a Bartlett tree surgeon advance man stopped in here to look around balefully, and I was just about to let him into my elm trees when I saw the female Baltimore oriole casing one of the elms, so I called off the deal. The orioles haven't been here since 1961, but a pair showed up about ten days ago and went straight for the old pear tree by the barn, which is the birds' saloon on this place.

Hope you are enjoying good health and the vernal season. Frozen water in Brooklin night before last.

Yrs.,
Whitey

May 30, 1964

Dear Whitey:

I hope you stood up well during the conferring of the day's honors at Colby and got home to North Brooklin and to bed at a wholesome hour. Are you going to put the medal on the terrace? You could sit out there after the black flies are gone, and glance at it between sips. A nice thing to picture, with the Tom Collins season coming up.

Yours of May 22—aside from its churlish attitude toward my remarkable pullets—heartens me with news of K's improvement. What a hell of a siege you went through.

Your score on books is ten more than mine, but you shouldn't lay off on nineteen. It's an odd number. If you brought out a twentieth, you could include "The Sea and the Wind That Blows," and get Bogey's boat-casket between two hard covers.

Our pullets that you excoriated scored 24 for 25 birds three days in a row and dropped back to 23 yesterday. If I could get a hold of the White automatic two-pail sanitary waterer you built for me, we might make a perfect score. I could drive up and get it some morning, or we could meet at Marion Village for lunch some day and make the transfer. I'll buy the lunch (Or how about coming to our plantation for an installation ceremony?).

We are pleased to pieces about the medal, Whitey. Congratulations from your South Bristol admirers.

Yours ever,
Smitty
Damariscotta, Maine

June 3, 1964

Your production figures not impressive. I have a hen with a fractured hip who can still lay and does. Thanks for letter. Medal now in drawer upstairs. I had it laid out on piano for three days, but visiting Republicans found it offensive. Will see that you get non-automatic pail waterer somehow or other. Right now Katharine is too sick for these adventures in husbandry.

Yrs.,
Whitey

On a typed blank postcard.

August 27, 1964

Dear Whitey:

Last word from you was a June 3 postcard snooting my egg production figures and bragging about your hen with the busted hip. My hens have no broken hips, and how a reliable poultry man would break a hen's hip is beyond me. Shame on you.

Ed Meyers saw the enclosed promotion from Harper-Atlantic Sales, Inc., and he wrote the red ink diatribe against their not including your name. I asked Ed's permission to send it to you as evidence of your faithful friends.

What is the Blue Hill mine going to do to you? Why are they putting copper mine residue in a Maine lake or pond? Don't they know copper sulphate kills things—like the cement-making discharge from the mill in Thomaston?

The swallows have gone. Our barn havened a couple of nests, and made me think of a line of yours: "a barn without a swallow is a tomb."

Been working gloomily on the pencil-pecking for my book, which is going to be titled, "Upriver and Down," and J. Donald Adams in writing a foreword; why, I don't know, except he wants to. I am in a fit of melancholy about the whole jeezely operation. It seems like double-stating, or over-stating, or just repetitious to me. But there's always the dough to consider. And I am crass enough, or needy enough, to consider it.

Speaking of considering dough, I got an assignment from my *Ford Times* bosses some weeks ago to write the lead story for the December (Christmas) issue. The subject: "A childhood memory of Christmas." It was quite an honor, so I blithely accepted. And I dislike children, Christmas, and the temp. was around 85 degrees. Moreover, I suppose I must have written—man and boy—at least a hundred Christmas stories and editorial bits. The thing came off to the extent of three enthusiastic telephone calls from Dearborn. And I am a fair-haired boy out there—but I hardly dare sign the piece. Iowa never saw corn to match it. Neither did Tiny Tim.

We are planning a winter trip to Bishop, Cal., to see our four grandsons. Son Jim and daughter-in-law, Avis, want to rendezvous at Las Vegas. I fear no good will come of it. It's in the Last Fling Department. One more poker game for Smitty, right in the John Oakhurst country. Your deal, suh.

Yrs.,
Smitty

P.S. A great year for Mary's garden lettuces. See next Sunday's *Portland Telegram*. Smitty.

North Brooklin
31 Aug. 1964

Dear Smitty:

That list of medalists was the 1964 crop selected by Lyndon Baines Johnson, probably with help from Luci. I was a member of the 1963 crowd, picked by the late John Fitzgerald Kennedy, with help from Jacqueline. I made it on looks alone. The medal is very pretty and I will wear it when I deliver your non-automatic waterer some day.

The Black Hawk Mining outfit has a license to put a shaft five hundred feet into the ground near Second Pond, sometimes called Douglas Pond. I attended the ceremonies that marked the opening of the mining operation and the death of the pond. The day was bright, and the pond had everything that I remembered from my earliest days in Maine, which were pond-side days. The pond will completely disappear during the course of the mining operation—it will get filled up with whatever comes out of the shaft. This will probably, in turn, go downstream to First Pond, sometimes called Billings Pond. Thence into the Salt Pond, thence into Blue Hill Bay. This is known as progress. The governor set off the charge of dynamite, and Representative Clifford McIntyre made a speech of cheer. I wept a small tear for the pond and went away.

K hasn't been able to shake the skin ailment that made her so sick. We're leaving here on Labor Day, headed for New York by easy stages, as she can't travel far in a day. We hope to be back after about two weeks of doctoring and dentistry. When I get some cheerful news I will hurry it along to you.

Yrs.,
Whitey

December 7, 1964

Dear Whitey:

Crows digging in the snow for apples under our old trees. Their feathers are puffed up in the cold so they look as big as capercaillies. The driving is unpleasant. My car wants to go sideways, either direction. I feel as if I were riding on a half-inflated basketball.

I sent the corrected galleys of my book to Holt, Rinehart & Winston the other day. I noticed a loss of zest in the operation, probably due to age. I'm about to be sixty-four and starting my Social Security year.

We were up to Colby one night in October to see the art exhibit and hear David McCord open the Gannett lecture series. He talked wittily and well on the general subject of light verse. Afterwards we had a few snorts with the Striders at their house, and they and Dave had a lot of nice things to say about you. Next day, Dave was down to our house for the afternoon—a lot of anecdotes about Copey, Bliss Perry, and other Cambridge characters we once knew and still revere.

How was your September N.Y. trip? And did K's dermatitis clear up OK?

We are getting cold feet about going to California to see the kids. Planes make us unhappy. We can't find a travel agency that will handle reservations on domestic railroads; and besides, the last time we went to California by train we got blizzard-bound in Pine Bluffs, Wyoming, for five days. We'll probably spend the winter here in meditation.

Are you and K. off for the bayou? Hope you are both well, and that the new mine isn't too close to home.

Yrs.,
Smitty
Damariscotta, Maine

P.S. Just added a new name to our name-dropping inventory—
Mr. and Mrs. Robert Montgomery. Until garden freeze-up, they
were down from North Haven each week to Gay's store to lay in
a supply of Mary's fancy lettuces. Monty (as I have not yet called
him) says: "This is the best time of year in Maine—no people."
Good for him.

January 25, 1965

Dear Whitey:

Your last dateline was Tidalholm, Beaufort, S.C. Where Sam Adams used to hang out. I hope you live as long as Sam did on one leg.

The Adventures of Tom Sawyer, of Damariscotta, Maine, are recorded as follows:

(1) I am the only living man whose wife gave him a telephone pole for Christmas. Around 23 December, '64, Mary drove the wagon into the barn where I was working on a piece of furniture, and she said: "Come look, your present." The wagon was loaded solid with six-foot chunks of a cedar pole that must have weathered under the aegis of the Nash Telephone people and their helpmates, the Central Maine Power people, for thirty years. The pole was nearly sixteen inches at the butt, and I sawed (bucksaw, kid) fifteen-inch lengths off it, and split off kindling. It flaked like cedar shakes with mallet and frow, and it sang like a xylophone under the touch of my inspired axe. Mary gave me the pole to remind us of our cabin days in the remote places, when the smell of cedar kindling taking flame was a sense of security. And defiance, too. This cedar is extra, because we wonder what was said to and by whom over the wires that were strung from it. Speculation as to this led to some extra drinks before supper on a night or two.

(2) We are home last Friday at sunset from a five-day trip to New York. We were so spleeny about flying, and both of us have done a lot of it, that we advanced on New York via bus and railroad.

We were so scared of New York that we dusted out via plane and reached Portland in two hours. Home is heaven.

(3) The N. Y. trip had a purpose. We were to appear—me in tuxedo, Mary in long dress—to see Justice Bill Douglas receive an award from the Camp Fire Club of America. The reason we were invited to attend was that I had influenced Justice Bill to accept the award. Mary bought the long, white dress, I rented the black tie combo, and we wound up at the head table, on the Lion's right hand, his new bride on his left. Several whiskies made this seem every-day to me, and we took bows when introduced as though we had shot big game and liked it. The banquet hall sounded like an apiary on fire, and we left at eleven p.m. Three hours past our home deadline. Douglas's new wife, Joanie, is lovely; and Bill himself looks ten years younger than when we saw him last.

(4) The "Please Call at Window" card this morning at the P.O. brought me a steam-heated, air-conditioned, 3-lb. volume called *Values in Literature*. The god-damnedest textbook I ever saw. Beautiful color reproductions of a lot of beautiful paintings—everything visual, and catalogued. If I'd had a textbook like that in prep, or high, I might of got educated. But I might not of. Because along with the great guys and girls, living or dead, I find you on page 418, me on page 46, and what are the school children going to think of us?

My piece is an honest thing about crawling through a sewer pipe. Yours is an equally miserable thing about hens. I have just now read them both, with the horror about even.

We are so glad to be home after New York that I am a little whacky. Am sure you will understand and condone.

So just lie back quietly at Tidalholm, and think of *Values in Literature*, Houlton Mifflin Company, Boston, New York, Atlanta, Geneva, Illinois, Dallas, Palo Alto. Weight, five lbs. We get around, Whitey.

What's happened to *you?*

Yours ever,

~~Tom Sawyer Smith~~
Smitty
Damariscotta, Maine

P.S. Who makes all the scratch from these big textbooks we authors actually write? Why don't we get out one of our own and rake in the shekels. We could get up one for adolescents and call it *The Acne Anthology.*

Sarasota
Feb. 15, 1965

Dear Smitty:

The last time a telephone pole collapsed in front of our house, we sneaked out under cover of darkness and hacked it up. We left Tidalholm and proceeded to Fiddler Bayou—Katherine is still fighting the skin malady that makes life fairly unendurable.

Whitey

On a hand-written blank postcard.

May 4, 1965

Dear Whitey:

The swallows have returned to our barn, so I know you must be back home from the Bayou. Two good friends of mine, John Ives Sewall and James H. Herbert, were to North Brooklin the other day and visited your son, Joel's, boatyard. They tell me it is a fine one. My own boatyard is in the barn. It harbors one Old Town guide's model canoe that I hardly dare sail anymore. I mean, paddle and pole. I'm not the balanced man I used to be.

Artist Maurice "Jake" Day, and his wife, Martha, have carved a lot of black-capped chickadees and mounted them in characteristic poses on weathered driftwood. Jake is an old friend of mine, and his Katahdin watercolors are sound documents of our northern wilderness. When I saw his chickadees, I went exploring in old *Ford Times*es to find your statement on our state bird under the Charles Harper design. In case you don't remember it, I enclose the card Jake designed, which quotes it. If Jake happens to like the person buying a mounted chickadee, he slips them a card.

As a result of researching your chickadee cameo in the *Ford* magazine, it occurred to me that you might have a slim volume all written. You wrote twenty of these 65-word memos for the *Ford Times*, and they are too good to let sleep if they would be children and their parents wake up. Seems to me some good publisher would grab the White birdsong with appropriate illustrations in four colors—either the Harper originals, or someone else's, especially done. You said you have nineteen books, and you were through with books—your own, I mean. This might be one you wrote and forgot. I can get you copies of your bird remarks, if you haven't got them on file. They are damn good,

Whitey, and I think the idea of a slim, terse volume might appeal to people, big and little. The book rights, of course, are all yours, unless I've missed some fine print somewhere.

I asked my publisher (Holt, Rinehart & Winston) to send you a copy of *Upriver and Down*, by me. That's on account I owe you a book trade for *Points of My Compass*. *Upriver and Down* is only my tenth book. Maybe there is something to be said for Henry Beston, who wrote one and lives happily ever after—a great Thespian.

At this writing—or instant—Mary has forty-nine 75-foot rows of garden stuff planted and transplanted. If this letter goes on another half-hour, the score will go up several rows. She moves fast. I am slowing up. It's pleasant.

What about you and yours and everything?

Your pal,
Smitty

P.S. Hardly dare mention the occupants of the White Correspondence School henhouse. They are doing too well.—S.

16 May 1965

Dear Smitty:

If Mary has a lot of stuff in the garden you must live in a softer climate than ours in Brooklin. We're still digging out after the winter. The frogs keep talking about spring, but night before last I thought it was going to snow.

The day your letter arrived, I was too busy to open my mail. My daughter-in-law managed to run over and kill a woodcock hen that was taking her chicks across the highway. This was in the morning. I walked back to the scene of the accident and found two chicks crouched obediently just off the shoulder. They were about the size of a standard hen's egg and had long bills just like a woodcock, only made of rubber, like a fake dagger. I picked them up, walked back to the house with them, and installed them in a box behind the wood stove. I then boned up on woodcock in Forbush, dug a few worms, and began the ridiculous task of keeping two wild chicks alive by force-feeding them. I stayed with this crazy work all day, and by nightfall the chicks were very active and alert, but I was exhausted. I was then faced with the decision whether to take them to bed with me, or find a broody bantam hen, or contrive a small brooder. Then I remembered that I still had a makeshift brooder left from a springtime when I mothered a lone gosling, so I put them in that. They didn't feel at home, though, and the light shone from the top of the tin can where the 25-watt bulb dangled. By bedtime, the contraption was so hot I didn't dare go to sleep; so I installed a weaker bulb. It was too weak, and in the morning the chicks were dead, having chilled in the night. They were the prettiest little things you ever saw.

Thanks for the suggestion about a book of birds. I have the copies of the *Ford* magazine, and will read the descriptions over when I get a chance. There's an idea in it, but I don't know that I want to pursue it at the moment. Incidentally, if Jake Day is passing out chickadee cards along with the sale of carved birds, isn't there some question of copyright involved? It's a small bird and a small matter, but I have a feeling that there is some small violation, if money is changing hands. Don't go scaring Jake Day about this, as I am not in an ugly mood and am just curious to know whether *you* know what the legal proprieties are in such cases. We aging authors have to keep mending fence, you know.

Thanks, too, for sending me your tenth book. I am in the middle of *The Treasure of Our Tongue* by Lincoln Barnett, and *Upriver and Down* is next on my list. The English language is a wilderness, and I'm sure your stories are wilderness stories, so I am having a wild, wild binge.

There was a Glossy Ibis in the pond by the Blue Hill golf course last week. I thought it was clever of me to discover him. I had never seen one before and had to come home and consult Peterson in order to find out what I'd been looking at. But on Christmas Day, in Yemassee, South Carolina, I saw a flock of 19 White Ibises come to roost in a dead tree—a brave sight.

Yrs.,
Whitey

May 18, 1965

Dear Whitey:

Yours of the 16th about the woodcock to hand. What a harrowing episode of life and death. You're the only man I know whoever worked that close with baby woodcock. You made a hell of a fine try.

I was up in the lake-and-forest country a few days. I spent most of them on my bunk in a log cabin wracked with fever. What I had was erysipelas, and I would have preferred just the plain sipelas. The whole right side of my head looked like a poison boxing glove, my ear like a boiled lobster claw. A pal drove me home in my car, and Mary put me to bed, and Doc Bostwick came down with a satchel of wonder drugs which cleared up the mess in three days. I'm okay now, but peeling, like after a bad sunburn.

Mary's X-thousand transplanted lettuce seedlings are treading water, holding their own, but that's about all. She is not baffled, or even discouraged. She replaces the drop-outs and looks to the sky for sun, a woman born to the soil.

About Jake Day's chickadee card: I think you have some kind of copyright point. The idea of the card was all mine, and so, therefore, is the blame. It never occurred to me at the time as having a commercial aspect. I don't suppose Jakey would give out as many as a hundred cards, one per chickadee carving. But, small as it is, the precedent is bum. Maybe it's something for Justice Bill Douglas to settle. Here are some suggestions from me:

1. A Cease and desist order, which would wipe it all out clean. I don't know what Jakey's expense for printed cards was, but I could take care of that since I started the whole thing.

2. A royalty to you of so much per card handed out to chickadee-buyers.
3. Let the whole thing ride, as is, but with a specified time limit—say November 1, 1965.
4. Put the matter into the hands of your literary agent.
5. You settle with Jakey—or he with you—for one Top Grade chickadee mounting, retail value about fifteen bucks, in exchange for the right to use the cards for the year 1965 only.

So help me, I never dreamed I was off base. But that's no excuse. I won't say anything to Jakey till I hear from you.

Ever your friend,
Smitty

P.S. Whitey: Don't put that bird-caption book too far back on the shelf. I am full of faith in it. It would be restful work for you this summer, in between saving birds' lives and spotting Glossy Ibises. Smitty

20 May 1965

Dear Smitty:

Sorry to hear of your erysipelas. My wife's father had it once and damned near died. He got his on a train. I will probably get mine from handling your letter, but I'm ready for anything these days. Just threw my hip out building a rabbit hutch for a grandson. I was doing all right until I tried to climb into the hutch to execute a particularly difficult maneuver of toenailing. Stay out of rabbit hutches if you know what's good for you. Today I'm in a corset and can't tie my shoes because I can't reach that far.

Don't worry about Jake Day's little cards. I think cease and desist would be the best course. I don't want any money, and I'm not even sure I have any rights in the matter anyway, as I don't recall how my agreement with the *Ford Times* read. Maybe he could get permission from them to use the material, but I do think he needs *somebody's* permission, since it is copyrighted material and he is using it in connection with sales of a product.

We got about an inch of rain in the last three days, and in another couple of hours we will get a burst of sunlight—which I will try to deflect onto my left hip. A bluebird stopped by here about ten days ago, took a drink from my pear tree, and beat it. I think the size of my swallow population gave him the bends, but he may be back if he can find a woman.

One of the grain stores in Ellsworth has some Mallard ducklings and I am thinking of buying two of them to take the place of my lost woodcock chicks. I also need a puppy, if you know of a puppy. My dog died last fall. I need a collie-cross that will chase only late-model cars.

Yrs.,
Whitey

May 24, 1965

Dear Whitey:

Jakey and his wife, Martha, are up in the mountains of Baxter Park. They are out of communication; but I'll tell Jake about the cease and desist when he gets back. It's a cinch they're not selling any chickadees or passing out the little cards—not where they are now.

Sorry to hear about your bout with the rabbit hutch. I am not too sympathetic with your trouble tying shoelaces. A man your age should be wearing slippers. I use Bean's canoe shoes, slippers with a zipper. I get them large enough so I can get out of them and into them without un-zipping. Very comfortable and convenient.

Did you ever see a copy of *Values in Literature*, Houghton Mifflin? I was looking through it again the other day, and it's some book. Outside of us being in it (I under the name Edmund Ware) along with other celebrated writers, the color illustrations are practically suited for framing. Your neighbor (once my neighbor in Northhampton) is one of the editors—Mary Ellen Chase.

Are you serious about the dog? Jake Day's son McClure is our local vet. Mac often has nice dogs to give away, all varieties. If you want me to put Mac on the dog trail, tell me, and the make and model of your car you want chased, and I'll pass the word to McClure.

Yrs.,
Smitty

Friday, June 9, 1965

Dear Smitty:

I have been sick and am behind on correspondence and other things. Am going up to the hospital this afternoon to find out whether my heart is still beating.

I received a note from Maurice and Martha Day, with one of the chickadee carvings. Will you please thank them for me when you see them. I will try to write later. I take it that they plan to continue passing out the cards even though I don't want them to do this. What I can't understand is why the *Ford Times* gave the permission for this kind of use without consulting me, and I'd like to write to somebody at the *Times* if you will give me a name. I've forgotten the name of the fellow I used to correspond with.

Whitey

June 11, 1965

Dear Whitey:

A letter from F. W. Fairfield, Manager, Consumer Publications, says, ". . . Jake Day has the permission of the *Ford Times* to use the quotation on the card that accompanies his hand-carved chickadees. If this doesn't take care of the problem, let me know." Fairfield's letter was dated June 4. If there is any further doubt, maybe you'd better write Fairfield direct, since I no longer have any powers at the *Ford Times*. However, Jake now has the official permission, which I gather is what gnawed at you. Hope it's okay.

Drier than hell here. Hauling water for the lettuce plantation. Trying to get plumbers to install a pump is hard hunting. Shot a woodchuck the other day while he was working down a spinach row. A very unpleasant experience for both of us.

Yours,
Smitty
Damariscotta, Maine

Sabbath
July 11, 1965

Dear Whitey:

I am distressed that you are sick and in the hospital, and hope your heart beats on and on. Mine stops for several minutes on Saturday nights, but picks up again on Sunday. I like to give it a rest once a week.

And I am distressed about the chickadees and cards, because you are. I am also distressed because I am the guy who suggested the crime but did not commit it. So I am kind of Fagin.

Jake and Martha Day are acting in good faith, feeling that the *Ford Times* permission to use the cards makes it okay. One of your letters to me said there should be a *Ford Times* permission, and the *Ford Times* gave it. Apparently, the Dearborn boys figured that did it. And so did Jake and Martha.

But I don't like it, and you don't, and the mistake—the bad manners, at least—was in not asking you first. This you have pointed out in yours of Friday, June 9th.

The thing started on my impulse to have Jake's chickadees described and explained in a few words—yours. I should have kept my trap shut. Another distress note. I hate to see it build up to woe, when it started off innocent.

The guys involved, except me, are gentlemen and ladies. The gentleman to correspond with at *Ford Times*, is:

Frederic W. Fairfield, Editorial Director
Ford Times
The American Road
Dearborn, Michigan

I sent Fred some excerpts from our letters (yours and mine) about the cards and chickadees, but none of our private stuff. So tell him how you feel, Whitey. I feel awful. Hope you don't.

Yrs.,
Smitty

August 16, 1965

Dear Smitty:

The battle of the chickadee cards is over, and the smell of smoke lingers in the air. I have never been sure that you and Day understood what the shooting was all about, but I saw no reason to back down merely because it involved a friend and a bird who is also a friend. The issue was clear-cut: Use of my name in connection with the sale of a product, or promotion of same, and I took a stand on this question about forty years ago and have not budged from my position, which was Nix. Am still mounted on my precarious little pinnacle, waving my stuffy little flag, and you boys should salute when you go by. Hell, I could have been promoting everything from puppy biscuits to toy mice, at wonderful gain to my pocket, if I had chosen to join the procession.

Your new stationery is fine, but the dollar-a-year wage is out of date. What with inflation it should be at least three dollars, plus carfare.

I am not well, but I am well enough. I have dizzy spells, sudden loss of vision, and a disinclination to go anywhere, do anything, or speak to anybody. The spring that supplies my house still has some water in it, but the pond in the pasture is mostly green scum. I have two Mallards poking about in the scum, and I have a black and white puppy who can carry a 4-quart measure by the bail. Or is it bale?

Yrs.,
Whitey

December 17, 1965

Dear Whitey:

Since your last note—the one putting the chickadees to bed—
we have been to Bishop, California, to see my son, daughter-in-
law, and four grandsons; and we have acquired, via two bulldoz-
ers (one got stuck), a farm pond seven feet three inches deep,
and in area about like Yankee Stadium. I don't know which is the
richer experience—richer to me, the bulldozer crew, or United
Airlines. One of us is broke.

The flight to Las Vegas (from Boston) where my son met us and
drove over Westguard Pass to Bishop, was terrific. My wife won
eighteen bucks in the Las Vegas gaming hells. Coming and going,
we saw Bryce Canyon, Zion National Park, and the Grand Canyon, all looking spectacular at 39,000 feet below the jet, which,
according to the captain, was traveling at 600 m.p.h. I didn't
doubt him. But it was hard to believe the temperature outside
the plane was 79 degrees below zero. I didn't get out to verify it.
I still remain uneasy in flight. I belong on the ground. But the
United Airlines people alleviate your uneasiness with bourbon
and champagne and smooth out the turbulence, if any. It was
nice to get on land again at Boston, and into a good, motionless
bed in the Ritz Carlton. The bed, medium priced, cost $27.

The farm pond is our answer, a season late, to last summer's
drought. Next season, after we have our sprinklers installed and
pump working, it will doubtless rain every third day. But the
pond is lovely to look at, with pines and hackmatacks all around
and deer tracks on the clay banks. It's iced over now, with a few
inches of snow over the ice. We were just up there for a look,
and see where a rabbit made it across okay. He was making long
leaps, maybe being pursued from above by a hawk.

Where are you? And how are you? This is mainly to wish you and K. a Merry Christmas. And to wish myself one, too. My first Social Security check is due. If it comes, I'm going to blow it on wassail. If it doesn't, I'll go back to work.

Merry Christmas!

Smitty

Sarasota, Florida
19 January 1966

Dear Smitty:

You seem to be doing all the things I would *like* to be doing—building a farm pond and putting up overnight at the Boston Ritz. I have two chances to construct a pond: I could deepen the existing pasture pond, which I am loath to do, or I could dam my brook, which they tell me is the wrong way to go about making a pond but which beckons me. I wish people would quit warning me about doing wrong things and just let me go ahead.

I would like to see your pond sometime. Last summer I managed to raise some Mallard ducklings, and they soon discovered the pasture pond and were delighted with it.

But it was my luck to have the Great Drought of 1965 coincide with a duck enterprise. The pond, for the first time under my stewardship, dried up. The Mallards stuck with it to the bitter end and I didn't blame them a bit when they flew away, seeking wetter pastures.

We're down with the Senior Citizens again—a dopey life but it keeps K. afloat. We had to change from Fiddler Bayou to Bayou Louise when the house we've been occupying for the last several years became unavailable. This new location is pretty weird; the Bayou runs parallel to the Gulf and the two are separated, at this spot, by only about a hundred feet. I can spit out the kitchen window into the Bayou, and I can make it from the living room into the Gulf in two jumps. I have a dock in front and a dock in back. No boat. Fishing has turned out to be very good in the Bayou. On my third cast on my first day, I hooked a 25-inch redfish. He sashayed up and down the Bayou for ten or fifteen minutes while my wrist got the best workout it's ever had, and

I finally landed him by summoning my wife, who found a key to a forbidden locker and extracted a landing net belonging to the owner. Snook, trout, sheephead, and flounder also visit the Bayou. My chief trouble as a fisherman is that I don't care much for fishing. Prefer sailing and drinking. I don't sail anymore, so that leaves just drinking. And lately my throat has been bothering me and I'm too chicken to go to a doctor, so even drinking has lost its immediate charm.

We drove down. Made it in eleven days. And we'll probably drive back in April. You were the first person I ever saw use a seatbelt, when you drove out of our yard. I've finally come to it, but Katharine is still a holdout. She says it irritates her skin.

Yrs.,
Whitey

Sunday
January 30, 1966

Dear Whitey:

No matter how dopey the life at Bayou Louise, stay there. The life here is so un-dopey it's dangerous. We are in the midst of a blizzard—the second within a week—the likes of which I haven't seen except in the mountains. The snow is horizontal in an east-southeast wind gusting to sixty or better, according to the weather watchers. The poor bastids on the snowplows are exhausted and red-eyed from trying to find the contours of the road, and they are aching from trying to hold the wheel against the side-thrust of the plow blade. John Ridd, of *Lorna Doone* fame, was a chicken compared to our plow boys. A power failure is near certain. Mary and I have been wallowing, back to the wind, from house to barn, to load up wood boxes. We are trimming lamp wicks—an art that is about lost except to Senior Citizens.

The storm is marvelous to watch. Cyclonic twists of snow, like dust devils in the desert, rage across our back field, turn, dart insanely, and soar into the sky. Happily, the liquor cupboard is well stocked with Gordon's, S.S. Pierce No. Six, and some exotic stuff my wife has squirreled from the Christmas onslaught of gifts. I could drink for a month on what I am sure is in closets and under lingerie in various bureau drawers. A sweet security. Especially for an apprentice "Herzog." I have just finished *Herzog*. And I think it's the most uninhibited exercise in introspection and self-analysis ever published. The erudition overwhelmed me. Any erudition does.

I can absorb your attitude toward fishing. It doesn't excite you. I wear the scars of its past excitement. Memory. Filled waders. A hollow creel. Chill waters. Catarrh. An impassioned talk to an

Anglers' Club. Doubt. A wave of sympathy for the trout. But a distilled beauty of the stream as it curves and recoils through its rocks and roots. That's all for me, Whitey. Bag limit is a dirty term. So is "Senior Citizen." On the golf course, we have banned it in favor of "The Geriatrics Foursome." Everyone is scairt to get called old. Yet oldth has its compensations. You don't have to prove you're brave any more. You've already done it. So no more jumping off the highest roof, running the wildest rapids in a shallop. What we have, Whitey, is the divine recourse of the Jug. All you have to do is wait through the bayou fishing till around four o'clock. After that, there's tomorrow. I'm for that. Something good might happen.

Fasten your seatbelt, Whitey. It will give you confidence and hold your spine in shape. If a cop stops you, tell him, "Nobody has been drinking except the driver."

See you in jail, affectionately,
Norman Vincent Peak

February 7, 1966

Dear Whitey:

We saw *Stuart* last night, but not in living color, as we have only a gray and white TV machine. Even in these drab shades, it was appealing. Pleased to note from Stuart's bedroom wall decorations that he is a Cornell mouse. We especially liked the air-sea rescue and class room scenes. Not so sure about the segregation policy on cats. Possible Bill of Rights violation here. But the North-in-Spring theme is fully subscribed. See that you follow it.

Also, go out and buy a current (March) *Field & Stream* magazine and read "Legend of the Pink Lady," by Smitty.

Ed Myers reports you have a piece about Forbush in a recent *New Yorker.* I am chasing it down. Could this Forbush business mean you are thinking about that bird book?

Yrs.,
Smitty
Damariscotta, Maine

Sarasota
February 25, 1966

Thanks for the picture of your henhouse in living color. Sent in my chick order this morning to Hall Bros, for May 2 delivery. Met a man who spotted my Maine license plates and asked where I lived. I said Brooklin. "What about White, is he dead?" he asked.

Whitey

On a hand-written blank postcard.

February 28, 1966

Dear Whitey:

Your card in hand. It's frustrating. What did you say to the guy who said to you, "What about White? Is he dead?"

The guy asked you a straight question. He wanted an answer. You have not revealed what it was. What was it? What is it? I think the answers would make interesting reading, or writing, or even arithmetic.

I am still heavy with snow shovel. But the big drifts are wasting fast, and the mud is just down there waiting to get tracked into the farmstead parlor.

Ever yours,
Smitty

Sunday, 1967

Dear Smitty:

It occurred to me the other day that you will have to quit calling me Whitey, as the name has come to be a term of opprobrium in Black Power circles. From now on you can call me Butch, or any other name you please.

How is life in Damariscotta among all those lettuce plants? I picked this summer to acquire a new boat—a 20-foot sloop named *Martha*—but on most of the days I could just barely see the bowsprit from the taffrail, and I had to lay out a compass course in order to row ashore. The boat is great, though. Steady as a scow. My granddaughter christened it with a bottle of Piper Heidsieck in full view of the entire Junior High School, who were let out of school for the occasion. I still love to sail, despite my many instabilities and infirmities. When I go alone, I stream my dinghy about a quarter of a mile astern, so that when I fall overboard I will surface in plenty of time to crawl aboard. This is assuming, of course, that I can still pull myself up over the stern of a small boat in wet clothes, a highly dubious assumption.

I think next summer will see Maine without a single tourist, so strong will be the memory of the great fog mull of 1967.

Yrs. thickly,
Andy White

P.S. Snapshot shows owner of the sloop *Martha* haranguing the crowd just prior to the launch. Note dolphins on the trailboard.

August 29, 1967

Dear Andrew:

Would have answered before, but I've been in hospital (what happened to the "the?") for 18 days with lung cancer. I am so full of cobalt, hydrogen mustard, and methotrexate, that I feel like a Class 5 fire hazard.

Had ahold of death's door a couple of times, but was not admitted. Spirits fine; getting best of care at home with Mary.

It's wonderful about your new boat—I even like its name. You better trail another quarter mile of rope behind the dingy, in case you can't climb into it. After the "Farewell to Sailing" note in your article about the sea and wind, I am especially delighted with *Martha*.

Your comment on the fog duly noted. It's been great for the lettuce garden. There must have been quite a bit of it around when they took that picture of you on *Martha*'s deck.

This is dictated to Mary and any mistakes are her fault.

Gallantly,
Cobalt Smith

North Brooklin
13 Sept. 1967

Dear Smitty:

I was distressed to hear your news, and would have sent off a letter sooner but haven't been too sharp myself of late—my head seems increasingly to be stuffed with old tomato paste and wired for sound. But, as a writer in the *Ellsworth American* remarked recently, "to all *intensive* purposes" I am all right. Nothing that a good blow with an 8-pound striking hammer wouldn't cure.

About twenty years ago one of my brothers went through pretty much what you have been going through, except that in those days I don't think cobalt got into the act. His cancer was not only arrested but as far as I know it was exterminated, like any rat. He is ten years (no, I guess it's eight) older than I am, and is fine. Thrashes about all over the place and still does some teaching. I have every confidence that you will continue to thrash. And one of my friends here in Brooklin has been swallowing pills for the last couple of years (hormone pills) for prostatic cancer, and except for his developing a frontal system rivaling Jayne Mansfield's, of blessed memory, he is very well and is enjoying life—which consists to a high degree, in his case, of lukewarm martinis. I cite these case histories for your edification and encouragement; it would appear that the doctors (clowns) are really making some progress in this field.

My pretty wife is off to the hair parlor in Ellsworth, and I am spending this pretty morning writing long overdue letters, when I should be out on Eggemoggin Reach in my pretty sloop *Martha*—the one with the brown sails. I keep a bottle of Newburyport rum in a locker under one of the berths, and when my head is too jumpy for sailing I go aboard and drink. There is more than one way to skin a cat. My next letter will be to Dr. Frank Sullivan, the sage of Saratoga Springs, who, at age seventy-five or thereabouts, finally had a race named for him at the Saratoga track—"The Sullivan." I mailed him two dollars in advance of the event, hoping I could get a bet down on the winning horse, but the money got there too late. Frank himself managed to get a bet on the winner by the simple process of buying a ticket on every entry. Cost him only sixteen dollars, of which recovered about four. Frank's letter to me said that he is now enfeebled, turning gradually to stone, and can "only walk a few blocks." I shall advise him to quit walking and break into a trot, the way I do—challenge is the thing at our age.

All the best to you and Mary
Yrs.,
Andy

Edmund Ware Smith died shortly after receiving this last letter in 1967. His wife, Mary, survived him for thirteen years.

April 11, 1980

Dear Mr. Myers:

Thank you for your letter, with its sad ending. I am sorry that you have lost such a good friend as Mary Smith. This world can use more like her.

If the Damariscotta Library is well established and intimately entwined with Edmund and his Rangers, it seems to me a good place for the letters to be. May they rest in peace and afford pleasure to readers!

Sincerely,
E. B. White

The Hen: An Appreciation

INTRODUCTION TO
A BASIC CHICKEN GUIDE FOR THE SMALL FLOCK OWNER BY ROY E. JONES (1944)

—E. B. WHITE

CHICKENS DO NOT ALWAYS ENJOY an honorable position among city-bred people, although the egg, I notice, goes on and on. Right now the hen is in favor. The war has deified her and she is the darling of the home front, fêted at the conference tables, praised in every smoking car, her girlish ways and curious habits the topic of many an excited husbandryman to whom yesterday she was a stranger without honor or allure.

My own attachment to the hen dates from 1907, and I have been faithful to her in my fashion. Ours has not always been an easy relationship to maintain. At first as a boy in a carefully zoned suburb, I had neighbors and police to reckon with; my chickens had to be as closely guarded as an underground newspaper. Latterly, as a man in the country, I have had my old friends in town to reckon with, most of whom regard the hen as a comic prop straight out of vaudeville. When I would return to the city haunts for a visit, these friends would greet me with a patronizing little smile and the withering question: "How are all the chickens?" Their scorn only increased my devotion to the hen. I remained loyal, as a man would be to a bride whom his family received with open ridicule. Now it is my turn to wear the smile, as I listen to the enthusiastic cackling of urbanites, who have suddenly taken up the hen socially and who fill the air with their newfound ecstasy and knowledge and the relative charms of the New Hampshire Red and the Laced Wyandotte. You would think, from their nervous cries of wonder and praise, that the hen was hatched yesterday in the suburbs of New York, instead of in the remote past in the jungles of India.

I am writing these preliminary remarks without having had the opportunity of reading what Mr. Jones, the author, has to say by way of instruction. To a man who keeps hens, all poultry lore is exciting and endlessly fascinating. I must have read millions of words of it over the years, and I am not tired yet. The subject seems to improve by much repetition. Every spring I settle down with my farm journal and read, with the same glazed expression on my face, the age-old story of how to prepare a brooder house—as a housemaid might read, with utter absorption, an article on how to make a bed.

Since this book is a guide, I feel I should instruct the reader, and should not only praise the hen but bury her. Luckily I can squeeze everything I know about chickens into a single paragraph, and it is presumably my duty to do so without further delay. Here, then, is my Basic Chicken Guide:

Be tidy. Be brave. Elevate all laying house feeders and waters twenty-two inches off the floor. Use U-shaped rather than

V-shaped feeders, fill them half full, and don't refill till they are empty. Walk, don't run. Never carry any strange object into the henhouse with you. Don't try to convey your enthusiasm for chickens to anyone else. Electricity is easier than coal, but an electric brooder should be equipped with a small fan in its apex to provide a down draft. Keep Rocks if you are a nervous man, Reds if you are a quiet one. Don't drop shingle nails on a brooder house floor. Never give day-old chicks starter mash for the first couple of days—give them chick feed, which is finely cracked grain. Don't start three hundred chicks if all you want is eight eggs a day for your own table. Don't brood with electricity unless you are willing to get out of bed at 3 a.m. for a thunderstorm and a blown fuse. Do all your thinking and planning backwards, starting with a sold egg, ending with a boughten starter. Don't keep chickens if you don't like chickens, or even if you don't like chicken manure. Always count your chickens before they are hatched. If you haven't got three hundred dollars and don't expect to have, don't buy three hundred day-old chicks, because you will soon need three hundred dollars. Use clean sawdust for nest material and renew it often. Never use straw for litter unless it is chopped. Tie your shoelaces in a double knot in the morning when you get dressed, since hens are under the impression that shoelaces are worms. When you move birds from a brooder house to a range shelter, keep them locked up in the shelter for two nights and one day before letting them out to play.

That is my basic guide. I have no doubt Mr. Jones should be consulted also, and I strongly advise you to read on.

A common charge made against a hen is that she is a silly creature. It is a false charge. A hen is an alarmist, but she is not silly. She has a strong sense of disaster, but many of her fears seem to me well founded: I have seen inexperienced people doing things around hens which, if I were a hen, would alarm me, too. Of course, the hen is intensely feminine. She is what the farmer calls "flighty," and this is particularly true of young pullets who are adjusting themselves to the severe strain of ovulation in the intoxicating days of early fall. Although I refuse to believe that she is a silly creature, I will admit that the hen is a rather unpredictable one and sometimes manages to surprise even on old friend and admirer like myself. Last December, after about sixteen weeks of collecting eggs in my laying house without causing any undue alarm among the birds, I went in one morning wearing a wristwatch which my wife had given me for Christmas. I opened the first deck of nests and thrust my hand in under a hen to pull the eggs out. The hen took one look at the watch and shrieked, "A time bomb!" Instantly the whole house was in an uproar, with hens trampling each other in a mad rush for the corners. This sort of panicky behavior causes some people to regard the hen as a silly creature.

Countless persons have had disastrous experiences with chickens—city persons who have imagined they could retire to the country and, with no previous training and no particular aptitude, make a nice living with hens. They might better have chosen dancing bears. The countryside is strewn with the crumbling ruins of their once golden adventure. Few people have any idea how much it costs to maintain chickens in the style to which they have been accustomed, how much and how varied the equipment required, how insatiable their appetite for grain, how many stages there are to the growth and development of a laying fowl, how easily the flock can be wiped out, how much labor is involved. It seems to me that anyone who proposes to go in for chickens, either as a wartime contribution or a peacetime venture, should start slowly and cautiously—not with a lot of new buildings and shiny fountains but with a few ready-made pullets from good stock. If chickens are to be merely a luxury fad, and you have money in your pants and want to erect a dream palace for hens and hire a governess to look after their wants and button them up, then that is a different story; but I am sure it is neither patriotic nor sensible to keep hens extravagantly, or ineptly, or at too great cost in materials and time.

In one matter I may be at variance with the author and publishers of this book, namely, the definition of a "small flock." My idea of a small flock is a flock of twelve. Or at most, eighteen. Anything over eighteen is not a small flock, in my opinion, but a big one. I know that a flock of two or three hundred birds is often spoken of as a small flock, and maybe it is, but I will let the reader answer for himself on the night in late spring when he comes in to bed after having transferred his three hundred young birds from their brooder houses to the range, picking each bird up in the darkness, loading it into a truck or wheelbarrow, transporting the living cargo to its destination, and then picking each bird up again and placing it darkly on the roosts. If after performing this nocturnal bit of husbandry he still thinks three hundred is a small flock, he is entitled to his opinion.

Keeping chickens, like any other year-round work, loses some of its original luster after long periods of it. But a man who really gets on close terms with hens is not apt to want escape. There are moments and days of discouragement: a hen on a sad morning making her sad noise and undoing your cleverest devices, can take the stuffing out of a man about as fast as anything I know. There are other moments and days which are richly rewarding and exhilarating. The feeling I had as a boy for the miracle of incubation, my respect for the strange calm of broodiness, and my awe at an egg pipped from within after twenty-one days of meditation and prayer—these have diminished but slightly. It was a city man, Clarence Day, who wrote:

> Oh who that ever lived and loved
> Can look upon an egg unmoved?

Surely that is the gentlest tribute and most exhausting sentiment ever written on this inexhaustible subject. Reader, if you can look upon an egg unmoved, stay away from hens!

Summer Hazard

—EDMUND WARE SMITH

A FEW YEARS GO, after long and heartful search, my wife and I found our permanent home and moved in, rejoicing. Hard by the soothing, old, sea town of Damariscotta on the Maine coast, our house is a restored Cape Codder with an ell; and we have a red barn with an amiable sag in its ridgepole. In all our years together, we had never owned a home except our log cabin; but now, in our middle fifties, at last we had one—with an old clock, fireplaces, a weathervane, a lawn mower, and two cats.

We went to work re-decorating and furnishing with a zeal which Mary called "the retarded nesting instinct." She had vast gardening projects, I vast writing projects. Together, we built pine cupboards, painted walls, sanded floors, and selected curtain materials. We bought a deep freeze in anticipation of Mary's garden produce; and I, myself, spent twenty-nine dollars for a waste basket just because it looked well in my study—a blissful extravagance you'd expect of a honeymooner.

There wasn't a cloud on our horizon till early the first Spring, when a revered neighbor told us in muted tones that, come summer, all would not be so idyllic. He spoke darkly of an annual, ninety-day siege—he used the word "scourge"—by something, or someone, called "they." As I remember it, the conversation went like this:

"How," asked our neighbor, "will you get any work done, when they find out where you are and start coming?"

"Who start coming?"

"Summer visitors. Dropper-inners."

"We haven't invited anyone, as yet."

"They spare you that detail," said our neighbor. "They simply arrive—with baggage."

"Who? Who are 'they'?"

"Friends, relatives, anyone you know or ever heard of—even total strangers."

"I don't believe it!"

"You will. It's a phenomenon—maybe not peculiar to the Maine coast, but especially virulent here. They hear you've got a nice little place. They want to share it with you during their summer vacation."

"But I'm not on vacation. I'm working."

"You won't be," said our neighbor, "not from June to September."

Feeling that this neighbor might be suffering from abnormal anxiety, we made further inquiry. All our informants corroborated the neighbor. Maurice "Jake" Day, artist friend, and long-time resident said:

"It's true. Wait and see."

"We could hang out a *No Vacancy* sign," I remarked, gaily.

"It's been tried," said Jake.

"How about *Closed for Repairs?*"

"That's the one you hang out in the fall, after they've all left."

We consulted still another resident, a man of much experience. He had very strong feelings on the matter.

"No policy or barricade ever invented," he said, "has success-fully repelled them. The only escape is to close your house, shutter it, erect tank traps in your driveway, and go visiting yourself, till after Labor Day."

As I look back on it, our friends Edward and Julia Myers, creators of Saltwater Farm, gave us the most poignant warning of all. Authorities on the subject of the casual summer visitor, Edward and Julie didn't say a word—just looked at us in sympathy, as upon dear friends about to undergo major surgery for the first time.

I regret to say that Mary and I regarded all these warnings lightly. We went on with our eager labors of home-making smug in the belief that our house was our castle.

This belief has been shattered. Far from being our castle—or even our *own*—our house at times resembled a small, free resort hotel, a rendezvous for the Corn Roast and Clam Bake Set, featuring exquisite cuisine and personalized service at any hour of day or night, with or without notice. We had never before enjoyed—or endured—such popularity.

At this writing, we have survived three, full-scale summer invasions by loved-ones and not-so-loved ones. And now, while convalescing from the third assault, I would review the experience in the hope of promoting a better understanding between our summer visitors and their host and hostess. The advice and observations offered are for the benefit and protection of both parties. Better human relations may result. On the other hand, they might cease entirely.

To begin with, if you should acquire a Maine coast home and a view, a deep dream of peace, and easy access to sea beaches, lobster pounds, a yacht club, and a golf course, let me suggest that you seal off, or de-activate, all spare bedrooms and padlock the liquor cupboard as a simple precaution against the unannounced house guests who "just happen to be driving up from Boston." In this way, you reduce your overall summer hazard to tent-pitching nieces and nephews, and old classmates traveling by in trailers.

You will find that the tent-pitchers require only lawn space and the use of your stove, refrigerator, automatic washer, clothesline, electric steam iron, and bathroom.

The trailer group, usually composed of whole families, is even more self-sustaining. They are often willing to settle for your electric current, water supply, and a patch of real estate under the shade of your old apple tree, if you'll just let them cut off those lower limbs so the trailer can get under.

"But," you say, "those limbs have little apples on them."

"Just green ones," replies your guest, swinging his axe.

As the fruited limbs fall upon the grass, you ask your friend how long he plans to be with you.

"A couple weeks," he says, "maybe three—depending on how the kids like it." And with a predatory glance at your wife's vegetable garden, he asks: "How's the sweet corn coming?"

During our first summer, I divided our visitors into two, broad classifications: My relatives, and my wife's relatives. This was a mistake. If one of my nieces regarded our telephone as God's gift in the field of free trans-continental communication, the fault was mine.

If one of Mary's nephews ravaged my beer supply and replaced it in the refrigerator with nursing bottles full of formula for his little son, I blamed Mary. Tempers flared for the first time in years.

"Don't you love little Bo—my own grandnephew?"

"Yes. But at times he's as damp and depressing as a flooded cellar."

"Don't talk that way! Besides, whose niece left us with a twenty-dollar telephone bill for calls to Los Angeles?"

We soon decided to abandon classification by relatives. The best method of typing, or classifying your summer visitors, is by their opening remarks, or entrance lines, as they swarm from their cars and dump the contents of their luggage compartments on your doorstep.

"You didn't answer our letter, so we just thought we'd surprise you."

Visitors using this approach are usually planning a four- or five-day sojourn. It won't do you any good to recommend a nice motel. Their arrival has been timed late in the day, when all the motels are booked solid. This type will settle in, and pervade and absorb your home. One or more of them will always be in the bathroom, and their medicines, cosmetics and suntan unguents will infiltrate the cabinets and shelves. They will remark that a fireplace fire is ever so cheerful, but under no circumstances would one of them think of bringing wood and kindling.

You will have trouble mowing your lawn except by night, for by day the shapely sun-bathers in this group lie about upon the sward, springing to life only at meal times.

"Oh darlings! We've had *such* a time finding you! We all want just a *teeny* peek at your lovely new home."

This type of entrance line may mean real trouble. Chances are you are in for some late poker games in which you will lose money. Breakfasts will be served individually from seven a.m. to two p.m. One of this party will probably sleep on the sofa in your living room, and you will step around him, or her, all morning. Another member of this set is very likely to ask you:

"What do you do all day?"

What you do all day, while they are at large on your premises and in your home, is to wait upon them and clean up after them. During a time of nervous exhaustion, I once told a visitor this. He thought it was a fine joke, and laughed loudly.

"You," he said, "are a card."

Another type of visitor says, on pulling into our driveway: "We're just stopping a moment. We don't want to bother you."

With this group, almost anything can happen. The suspense is terrific. They may, actually, stop a moment. They may, actually, not want to bother you. On the other hand, the slamming of their car door can toll the knell on you for ten days, with a possible repeat visit.

One gay, young party of nieces and nephews—mine and my wife's, in equal parts—took a look at our red barn that we had re-modeled and immediately planned to appropriate it for dancing. Refreshments, provided by us, would be served from a long, wooden bar, which I would build; and the orchestra would be composed of everyone from Satchmo Armstrong and Wild Bill Davidson to Jimmy Dorsey. I was so alarmed by the fierceness and sincerity of the young people's dream that I lost no time in filling the little barn with cordwood, rusty farm machinery, and old barrels.

Once, dizzy with fatigue after a visit from a family of four, including a teething babe—never mind whose relatives they were—I said to Mary: "Was it you who called this house 'our castle'?"

"It may have been."

"Castle! House by the side of the road, and let the world go by! 'Go by,' my eye! The world has beaten a path to our door. What we've got here is a better mouse trap."

I think it was soon after this, toward the end of our third season of philanthropy and short-order cooking, that I began to have hallucinatory conversations with guests. They were Walter Mittyish in tone and concept, and I would like to quote one or two of them.

"Look," I said—in fancy, of course—to an imperious young mother who had registered at our resort along with her husband and small children, "your husband works in an office, doesn't he?"

"Yes. What are you getting at?"

"Just this: Supposing I moved a crib into his office and loaded it with a live baby—and just left it there for a few days and nights?"

"That's different."

"Why is it different? He moved a crib, complete with a baby into my study, didn't he?"

"Our baby doesn't cry."

"He will when he wakes up and sees me at my desk."

"Oh, in that case, it will be your fault."

You see what I mean? You can't win, even in dreams. Another one of my Mitty dialogues goes like this:

"Why can't you spare us some time?" a young nephew asks me. "You're retired, aren't you?"

"What makes you think I've retired?"

"We never see you doing any work."

"No—and you never will; because the kind of work I do, you have to be alone to do it—just me and a typewriter."

For a moment, in my fantasy, I think I have scored heavily—but no—for my nephew says:

"Far be it from me to interfere, Uncle Edmund. Go ahead and get alone."

In almost any group of visitors, there is someone who gazes critically around our living room and says:

"*What?* No TV?"

When we explain that our budget is limited, and that we spent the TV money for power tools, this person usually snorts: "Who wants power tools?"

But perhaps the real infuriators are the amateur architects who wish to re-model our home, presumably for their own convenience.

"You ought to straighten out that sag in the barn ridgepole and put up a nice cupola with a light in it. You could have a room up there."

Or, "What I'd do would be to tear out the whole front wall of the house and put in plate glass all across it. Bring you right outdoors."

It has been suggested that a large, shed dormer would make room for two more, nice, airy bedrooms; that we ought to put a widow's walk on top of our house; that we erect a few circular turrets, glassed in. If we adopted half the architectural advice that has been offered to us, gratis, our home would resemble a child's nightmare of The Alhambra.

It was in the desperate last days of the 1958 summer hazard that I drew up a set of Rules and Regulations for use in governing the behavior of the casual visitor, whether friend, foe, or relative. Just the other day I came across the list. Oddly enough, it was tucked away among the pages of Harold Lamb's *The March of the Barbarians*. It reads as follows:

1. From prospective visitors, a clear statement in writing—preferably notarized—of arrival and departure times.
2. A complete inventory or members making up the party, including a statement of ages and sexes, and number of babies or toddlers.
3. A substantial deposit against breakage.
4. Mandatory: a house gift, or gifts, of food and beverage, the latter not to consist of milk for the very young.
5. A sworn statement to the effect that the applicants will make their own beds, empty ash trays, help with the dishes,

and stay out of the kitchen while the host and/or hostess are preparing meals.

6. No parking in the driveway.
7. A deposit of $5.00 (five dollars) for each book borrowed.
8. A severe fine for entering my study, with or without knocking, while I am in it.
9. Occupancy if the bathroom is limited to twenty minutes during the hours of eight to eleven, a.m.

Clearly, this list must have been written by a curmudgeon in a cold, white fury. But the curious thing is that as I re-read it, with the 1959 visiting season but a few months hence, I do not feel like a curmudgeon, nor can I evoke any sense of fury or diatribe. As a matter of fact, it is very lonely here in my study, and I wish a few nieces and some babies would drop in and pass the time of day. From my window I can see the apple tree from which my old classmate axed those lower limbs to admit his trailer. Good old George! That tree needed his pruning. It looks much better now.

By some strange, human phenomenon, I am pervaded by a feeling of warmth for old George and his Boy Scout axe, and this warmth slowly extends toward all the other guests, invited or otherwise. If we don't actually love these people, and long to see them again come summer, why did my wife ask me to build a little pine-paneled room in the ell of the barn? And why did I take such delight in building it? What visitor will first use the new room and when?

So it comes to pass that summer is not a hazard after all, but a hope. Perhaps this is one of the more striking examples of "Time heals all." Visitors, please come back! All is forgiven! Never mind about those Rules and Regulations. Just come. Will have TV— and maybe Hi-Fi, too. Open June to September. Completely re-decorated, but under same management.

Goodbye to Forty-Eighth Street

—E. B. WHITE

FOR SOME WEEKS NOW I have been engaged in dispersing the contents of this apartment, trying to persuade hundreds of inanimate objects to scatter and leave me alone. It is not a simple matter. I am impressed by the reluctance of one's worldly goods to go out again into the world. During September I kept hoping that some morning, as if by magic, all books, pictures, records, chairs, beds, curtains, lamps, china, glass, utensils, and keepsakes would drain away from around my feet, like the outgoing tide, leaving me standing silent on a bare beach. But this did not happen. My wife and I diligently sorted and discarded things from day to day, and packed other objects for the movers, but a six-room apartment holds as much paraphernalia as an aircraft carrier. You can whittle away at it, but to empty the place completely takes real ingenuity and great staying power.

On one of the mornings of disposal, a man from a second-hand bookstore visited us, bought several hundred books, and told us of the death of his brother, the word "cancer" exploding in the living room like a time bomb detonated by his grief. Even after he had departed with his heavy load, there seemed to be almost as many books as before, and twice as much sorrow.

Every morning when I left for work, I would take something in my hand and walk off with it, for deposit in the big municipal wire trash basket at the corner of Third, on the theory that the physical act of disposal was the real key to the problem. My wife, a strategist, knew better, and began quietly mobilizing the forces that would eventually put our goods to rout. A man could walk away for a thousand mornings carrying something with him to the corner and there would still be a home full of stuff. It is not possible to keep abreast of the normal tides of acquisition. A home is like a reservoir equipped with a gate valve: the valve permits influx but prevents outflow. Acquisition goes on night and day—smoothly, subtly, imperceptibly. I have no sharp taste for acquiring things, but it is not necessary to desire things in order to acquire them. Goods and chattels seek a man out; they find him even though his guard is up. Books and oddities arrive in the mail. Gifts arrive on anniversaries and fête days. Veterans send ball-point pens. Banks send memo books. If you happen to be a writer, readers send whatever may be cluttering up their own lives; I had a man once send me a chip of wood that showed the marks of a beaver's teeth. Someone dies, and a little trickle of indestructible memorabilia appears, to swell the flood. This steady influx is not counterbalanced by any comparable outgo.

Under ordinary circumstances, the only stuff that leaves a home is paper trash and garbage; everything else stays on and digs in. Lately we haven't spent our nights in the apartment; we are bivouacked in a hotel and just come here mornings to continue the work. Each of us has a costume. My wife steps into a cotton dress while I shift into midnight-blue tropical pants and bowling shoes. Then we buckle down again to the unending task.

All sorts of special problems arise during the days of disposal. Anyone who is willing to put his mind to it can get rid of a chair, say, but what about the trophy? Trophies are like leeches. The ones made of paper, such as a diploma from a school or a college, can be burned if you have the guts to light the match, but the ones made of bronze not only are indestructible but are almost impossible to throw away, because they usually carry your name, and a man doesn't like to throw away his good name, or even his bad one. Some busybody might find it. People differ in their approach to trophies, of course. In watching Edward R. Murrow's *Person to Person* program on television, I have seen several homes that contained a "trophy room," in which the celebrated pack rat of the house had assembled all his awards, so that they could give out the concentrated aroma of achievement whenever he wished to loiter in such an atmosphere. This is all very well if you enjoy the stale smell of success, but if a man doesn't care for that air he is in a real fix when disposal time comes up. One day a couple of weeks ago, I sat for a while staring moodily at a plaque that had entered my life largely as a result of some company's zest for promotion. It was bronze on walnut, heavy enough to make an anchor for a rowboat, but I didn't need a rowboat anchor, and this thing had my name on it. I finally succeeded, by deft work with a screwdriver, in prying the nameplate off; I pocketed this, and carried the mutilated remains to the corner, where the wire basket waited. The work exhausted me more than the labor for which the award was presented.

Another day, I found myself on a sofa between the chip of wood gnawed by the beaver and an honorary hood I had once worn in an academic procession. What I really needed at the moment was the beaver himself, to eat the hood. I shall never wear the hood again, but I have too weak a character to throw it away, and I do not doubt that it will tag along with me to the end of my days, not keeping me either warm or happy but occupying a bit of my attic space.

Right in the middle of dispersal, while the mournful rooms were still loaded with loot, I had a wonderful idea: we would shut the apartment, leave everything to soak for a while, and go to the Fryeburg Fair, in Maine, where we could sit under a tent at a cattle auction and watch somebody else trying to dispose of something. A fair, of course, is a dangerous spot if a man is hoping to avoid acquisition, and the truth is I came close to acquiring a very pretty whiteface heifer, safe in calf—which would have proved easily as burdensome as a chip of wood gnawed by a beaver. But Fryeburg is where some of my wife's ancestors lived, and is in the valley of Saco, looking west to the mountains, and the weather promised to be perfect, and the premium list of the Agricultural Society said "Should Any Day Be Stormy, the Exercises for That Day Will Be Postponed to the First Fair Day," and I would rather have a ringside seat at a cattle sale than a box at the opera, so we picked up and left town, deliberately overshooting Fryeburg by a hundred and seventy-five miles in order to sleep one night at home.

The day we spent at the Fryeburg Fair was the day the first little moon was launched by the new race of moon makers. Had I known in advance that a satellite was about to be added to my world, in this age of additives, I might have stayed in New York and sulked instead of going to the fair, but in my innocence I was able to enjoy a day watching the orbiting of trotting horses—an ancient terrestrial phenomenon that has given pleasure to unnumbered thousands. We attended the calf scramble, the pig scramble, and the baby beef auction; we ate lunch in the back seat of our flashy old 1949 automobile, parked in the infield; and then I found myself a ringside seat with my feet in the shavings at the Hereford sale, under the rattling tongue and inexorable hammer of auctioneer Dick Murray, enjoying the wild look in the whites of a cow's eyes.

The day had begun under the gray blanket of a fall overcast, but the sky soon cleared. Nobody had heard of the Russian moon. The wheels wheeled, the chairs spun, the cotton candy tinted the faces of children, the bright leaves tinted the woods and hills. A cluster of amplifiers spread the theme of love over everything and everybody; the mild breeze spread the dust over everything and everybody. Next morning, in the Lafeyette Hotel in Portland, I went down to breakfast and found May Craig looking solemn at one of the tables and Mr. Murray, the auctioneer, looking cheerful at another. The newspaper headlines told of the moon. At that hour of the morning, I could not take in the significance, if any, of a national heavenly body. But I was glad I had spent the last day of the natural firmament at the One Hundred and Seventh Annual Exhibition of the West Oxford Agricultural Society. I see nothing in space as promising as the view from a Ferris wheel.

But that was weeks ago. As I set here this afternoon in this disheveled room, surrounded by the boxes and bales that hold my un-disposable treasure, I feel the onset of melancholy. I look out onto 48th Street; one out of every ten passersby is familiar to me. After a dozen years of gazing idly at the passing show, I have assembled, quite unbeknownst to them, a cast of characters that I depend on. They are the nameless actors who have a daily walk-on part in my play—the greatest of dramas. I shall miss them all, them and their dogs. Even more, I think, I shall miss the garden out back—the wolf whistle of the starling, the summer-night murmur of the fountain; the cat, the vine, the sky, the willow. And the visiting birds of spring and fall—the small, shy birds that drop in for one drink and stay two weeks. Over a period of thirty years, I have occupied eight caves in New York, eight digs—four in the Village, one on Murray Hill, three in Turtle Bay. In New York, a citizen is likely to keep on the move, shopping for the perfect arrangement of rooms and vistas, changing his habitation according to fortune, whim, and need. And in every place he abandons he leaves something vital, it seems to me, and starts his new life somewhat less encrusted, like a lobster that has shed its skin and is for a time soft and vulnerable.

The Outermost Henhouse

—EDMUND WARE SMITH

I SHALL ALWAYS CONSIDER June 18, 1954, as Judgment Day for my wilderness life in Maine. As the forest surrounding our cabin awoke to birdsong, there was no premonition of change or disaster. The weather was clear, the track fast, and my wife and I sat down to the most delicious breakfast of our lives. It was also the most expensive.

The *pièce de résistance* was a chive omelet, and it was worth the price in its engendered complacency alone. The chives came from our cabin garden, and the eggs—all five of them—from our own white chickens which, as we breakfasted, were visible from the kitchen window in their yard extending from the Outermost Henhouse. "There never was an omelet like this," I remarked.

"Just think," said my wife. "We built the henhouse, brought the birds way back in here, and this feast is the result. More coffee?"

"Please."

A few minutes later, energized by omelet and coffee, and lulled by a false sense of achievement and well-being, I arose to write a business letter to a farmer acquaintance down on the Maine coast.

I never should have written that letter. A man with any reticence whatever would have limited a business letter to business; but, heady with success and beguiled by self-esteem, I got my business over in a paragraph and rushed on to the poetry, as follows:

Shin Pond, Maine
June 18, 1954

Dear Mr.——,

We live in this remote cabin six months a year, and spend the other six in the ghettos of Detroit, thus lending authority to those notes of yours on the blue jay, "a bird which doesn't seem to know whether to settle in a forest or a housing development."

On the path to our spring, a hermit thrush is nesting on four, brilliant, blue-green eggs, her eyes full of terrible fear as we pass with the water pail. But she is now getting used to us, although I do not wish to imply that we are trying to tame her. Her wildness is part of her wonder.

This year, for fun and fresh eggs, we have built—with due respect to our friend, Henry Beston—The Outermost Henhouse. No domestic egg was ever laid within thirty miles of this spot till a few days ago, when, in one of the nests, appeared a fine, brown ovoid about the size of a walnut. Estimating lumber, hardware, feed, and transportation of all materiél by pontoon airplane, we figure this morning's breakfast omelet cost $167.45. It was worth every penny.

We regard our White Rock pullets as a sorority, as select and refined a group of girls as you'd come across at Spence or Miss Porter's. The view from their playground is of Thoreau's Traveller Range across the lake, and the group seems content—except that one of them crowed one morning. A sex deviant in the dormitory. Lust was the order of the day.

With no presage of evil, I signed this letter and gave it to the care of The Birdman, the bush pilot who drops in ever and anon to see how we are faring. I thought no more about it, and my wife and I went on about our gardening, wood chopping, and work of life.

We had been told of a dread poultry disease called Blue Comb—that a tablespoon of molasses in a quart of water would ward it off. We dutifully followed this prescription, and the birds thrived. We had also been told that the presence of a rooster in our small group would tend to hinder the laying of eggs; and so, on a sad and harrowing day, we dispatched our rooster by means of a shotgun. A day later the game warden paid us a visit, saying he had heard we were shooting birds out of season. Following our explanation of the shooting, he stayed to dinner, which consisted mainly of the rooster.

Aside from this incident everything was peaceful and wilderness was paradise enough, till we went out one day to the tiny, forest hamlet of Shin Pond, and at the post office picked up our mail, which, unfortunately, included Mr.—'s reply to my all-but-forgotten letter:

Blank Town, Maine
June 24, 1954

Dear Mr. Smith,
From your letter it is plain to me that the end of your wilderness life is in sight. The domestic egg is the beginning of your doom, and I can see the whole pattern unfolding—first the henhouse, then the egg, then the grain bill, then the full corn in the ear, and the bulldozer to break trail for the grain truck, and at last the green lush pasture and the white-faced heifer bred by test tube arriving by Piper Cub because it's quicker than the truck. Ah wilderness! That first egg, so deceptively beautiful, so germinal! I bought this place because it had a good anchorage for a boat. One day I noticed it had a barn. Now I don't even have a boat.

Here in a single paragraph, our ten-year enterprise in wilderness living had been shaken to the core. On returning to the cabin, I re-read Mr.—'s letter and then walked up the path to The Outermost Henhouse. I found six warm, brown eggs in the nests which up to then was a near record for a single laying day. I spoke several kind words to the birds, whom we had now begun to call by name: Big Rosie, Stretch (who laid the huge double-yolkers), and Aunt Agnes. In both eggs and birds, in fact in the entire Outermost Henhouse project, there was no longer the full flow of satisfaction and joy. Mr.—, with his fell creep of omniscience, had got in his work. I could reply to him only as follows:

Dear Mr.—,
June 27, 1954—A six-egg day
Today we went the long, hard journey out to the settlements to buy beef steak, ten-penny nails, a whetstone, and some gin, only to find your depressing letter of June 24th prophesying the breakdown of my wilderness life. There is some evidence in support of your prediction of my doom. For it is true that The Outermost Henhouse was delivered piecemeal by Piper Cub. It is also true that Mr. Humpy Gould, the flying plumber, flies in to fix things we can't fix, which are several. Moreover, the eggs in the hermit thrush's nest are gone, and so is the creature herself—all gone, mysteriously, into the wilds.

Shortly after signing and sealing this letter, I read in the news how a renowned university had awarded an honorary degree to my Maine coast farmer friend. This intelligence came too late for me to tear open the envelope and write some appropriate congratulations. But the award seemed to give Mr.—'s views on everything, including my wilderness life, an added power and thrust. And one of the henhouse sorority, a thin girl named

Gladys, mysteriously died that very week. I began to dread the mail, but the reply to my letter inevitably came. I quote:

Dear Mr. Smith,
Was shocked to learn that you have plumbing at your cabin as well as eggs. And you're not kidding me about that gin, either. It wasn't just gin you bought out there in civilization; I am betting you *also* bought a bottle of dry vermouth or perhaps a small case of quinine water.
Never mind, I've just built a terrace. It cost three million dollars. You can see it from the little cove where I first dropped anchor so many years ago in the fog.
Yrs.,—

I was at first disarmed by what I felt was a lighter note in the above letter. But I was not long fooled. My correspondent was indeed relenting a little, but only because he knew he had me on the ropes. He was, in effect, walking to a neutral corner while the count was being taken.

Rallying, I rushed to my typewriter to compose the following:

Dear Mr.—,
July 3, 1954—A nine-egg day
My wilderness dream has again been nightmared by yours of June 30th. Several things need clearing up, including my plumbing. You need not be shocked by it, since it consists only of a sequestered privy overlooking the lake. On the back porch we have a gasoline pump which pumps water to the kitchen sink when it is in the mood. When it isn't, we get in touch with the Flying Plumber by Forest Service telephone. As I may have hinted, I am apprehensive about mechanical things, having but lately learned how to put a new blade in my safety razor without personal injury.

You also reached the wrong conclusion about my gin. I buy neither vermouth nor quinine water to pour on top of it, but Coca Cola. Is anything more uncivilized than that?

About your terrace, I admit being pretty impressed with its cost. But I shall be content with the rock walls my wife has constructed right here with the rocks she dug from the previously untrammeled wilderness. At this writing I value her at *more* than three million dollars, after taxes. There goes your terrace.

I thought this would block my opponent for a while, and it did. But not for the reason I thought, He had planted the seed, and he stood aloof and let it grow, as a Maine coast farmer should.

Whether from his planting, or from the subconscious desire he suspected occupied my mind, fine fruit has come; for in the spring of this year my wife and I bought a home full of fireplaces and modern plumbing down on the coast near Damariscotta, and there is a feeling we may withdraw there in time, tapering off our wilderness enterprise.

As for the occupants if The Outermost Henhouse, they are no more. Since we could not take them with us, we were obliged to eat them in the fall, feeling more than a little like cannibals as we did so.

Just before we crossed the lake in late October, I took a last look around at the closed and shuttered cabin. With mixed emotions, I noted several white neck-feathers adhering to the chopping block in the back dooryard. It was here that the guillotine had fallen. But, come early May, precocious robins would fly down to pluck and carry off these very feathers and with them line a nest in which to lay eggs which would hatch into little robins; and ere long the young birds together with their parents would fill the wilderness with the glory of song and new life—a thought my farmer friend would be the first to encourage and appreciate.

Acknowledgments

THANK YOU TO Martha White; White Literary, LLC and ICM Partners; and the heirs of Edmund Ware Smith for allowing the publication of these epistles. Thank you to Torie DeLisle for her enthusiasm in getting this project started. Thank you to Emily Meader for painstakingly transcribing and researching their contents. Thank you to Kathy McLauchlan, Skidompha Library staff genealogist, for inspiration and historical perspective. And thank you to Pam Gormley, Skidompha Library executive director, for recognizing the merit of a crazy idea. Thanks, also, to Jennifer Bunting for publishing advice and editorial guidance, and to everyone at Down East Books for their efforts to make this book a success.

Skidompha Library has been serving its community in Damariscotta, Maine, since 1882.